MW00513802

The Castle in the Pasture

The Castle in the Pasture

Portrait of Burr and Burton Academy

Burr and Burton Academy
Manchester, Vermont

First Edition

Published in the United States by
Burr and Burton Academy
Manchester, Vermont 05254

Text and research: Frederica Templeton
Concept and design: Doris Hardoon Woodward
Jacket design: Doris Hardoon Woodward
and Paris Woodward '02
Editor: Margot Page
Production Design: Greg Van Houten
Production Photography: Brian Gawlik

Color separations by Pre Tech Color, Wilder, Vermont
Printed and bound by CS Graphics Pte., Ltd., Singapore

ISBN: 0-9764711-0-8
Library of Congress Control Number: 2004099806

Foreword

It is hard to imagine today, after almost two centuries, how extraordinary an undertaking it was for the first trustees to establish an academy in a small frontier village. The townspeople called the new building "the castle in the pasture," perfectly expressing the endurance and permanence the founders sought for education in rural Vermont.

From its founding in 1829 to the celebration of its 175th anniversary, Burr and Burton Academy has nestled at the base of Equinox and cast its gaze upon the community it has served and which has supported it for nearly two centuries. The enduring partnership between Burr and Burton and the community remains the cornerstone of the school's success. An independent academy that provides equal educational opportunities for all students who reside in its tuition towns is indeed rare in today's educational landscape where schools are either entirely public or highly selective private institutions.

Burr and Burton remains true to its historical mission of enrolling all the students in our community while providing them with a rigorous and engaging academic program highlighted by a wealth of extracurricular and athletic options. Today, after 171 graduating classes have climbed the well-worn marble senior stairs at the entrance to Seminary Building, Burr and Burton is thriving. It is clearly the school of choice in an area of southern Vermont where the right to school choice is as ingrained in the culture as old barns, cow pastures, and maple syrup.

The community has responded to the school's unprecedented growth by enthusiastically supporting the funding for two major campus renovations in the last several years. While technology that our founders never could have imagined enriches every classroom and specialized programs address the broad diversity of students we enroll, Burr and Burton remains blessed because of the same passionate dedication of those pioneering teachers who greeted its first students back in 1832.

The school's history and its ties to its community come alive in the pages of this magnificent book which celebrates the 175th anniversary of one of New England's oldest and most venerable institutions. My heartfelt thanks to everyone who made *Castle in the Pasture: A Portrait of Burr and Burton Academy* possible; they indeed embody the community support and commitment generations have devoted to Burr and Burton Academy.

Charles W. Scranton
Headmaster
Burr and Burton Academy

Early lithograph of Manchester

*Bone of our bone, flesh of our flesh,
founded by our own merchants,
sustained for a hundred years chiefly by
the self-denying devotion of our citizens,
the Seminary is a symbol of our success.*

*Here is what our town can do: this
glorious old school. We have maintained
it against changing educational fashions;
against the cost of living; against the
universal vicissitudes of all experience,
for a hundred years as it was founded to
serve the children of this valley.*

Sarah Cleghorn
Class of 1895

KNOW ALL MEN BY THESE PRESENTS, That I Calvin P. Smith of Manchester

in consideration of the sum of Six Hundred & forty dollars, received to my full satisfaction, of Myron Clark Treasurer of Burr Seminary for & in behalf of said Corporation

the receipt whereof I do hereby acknowledge, have given, granted, bargained and sold, and by these presents do give, grant, bargain, sell, alien, release, convey and confirm unto the said Myron Clark Treasurer as afforesaid & to his Successors in Office ~~heirs and assigns~~, forever, a certain piece or parcel of land, situate, lying and being in Manchester aforesaid & described as follows, to wit, bounded Northerly by land owned by Frederick Smith, Ebenezer Chamberlain & Li. Sutherland Easterly by Land now in Possession of Man Roberts & Land of Wm Jameson Southerly by land of Elijah Collins, Westerly by Land of Major Hawley, Wm Rely Burr Smith & Aaron Baker Containing about One Hundred & fifty acres it being the Farm commonly called the Vaughan Farm

TO HAVE and to HOLD the said granted premises, with all the appurtenances thereof to the said Myron Clark Treasurer of Burr Seminary ~~heirs~~ and his Successors in Office ~~assigns~~, to his their own proper use, benefit and behoof forever. And I the said Calvin P. Smith do for my Self my heirs, executors and administrators, covenant to and with the said Burr Seminary ~~heirs, executors, administrators and assigns~~, that at and until the ensealing of these presents I am — well seized of the premises in fee simple; that I have a good right and lawful authority to bargain and sell the same in manner and form above written; that they are free and clear from all incumbrances; and that I — will warrant and defend the same against all lawful claims and demands of any person or persons whatsoever.

In witness whereof I *have hereunto set* my *hand and seal this* fifth *day of* September *Anno Domini One Thousand Eight Hundred and* thirty four

Deed for 150 acres sold to Burr Seminary trustees, 1834

Provided nevertheless, that if I the said Calvin P. Smith my heirs, executors or administrators, shall well and truly pay, or cause to be paid to the said ~~Myron Clark~~ Treasurer afforesaid & to his Successors ~~heirs, executors or administrators~~ in Office to & for the use of Burr Seminary the amount of a Promisory Note of said ~~Calvin~~ Calvin P. bearing even date he

Contents

Earliest photograph of Burr and Burton, 1867

I *Character & Discipline*

1829 - 1863

1829	Burr Seminary is incorporated by the Vermont State Legislature
1833	Burr Seminary opens on May 15
1837	The Reverend Joseph D. Wickham is appointed principal
1849	First young women are admitted to classes
1855	Trustee and founder Josiah Burton leaves bequest for female seminary
1860	Name is changed to Burr and Burton Seminary
1862	Burr and Burton closes for eighteen months for repairs and renovations

178

Dr Thomas Richardson Cr

Date	Day	Particulars	Fol.	£	s	d	Date	Day	Particulars	Fol.	£	s	d
1805 Decr	14	To Merchandize	543	1	1	—	1807 Sept	29	By Cash	531	1	10	2
1806 April	22	To do	70		18	—	Oct	10	By Wheat	546		7	2
June	25	To do	136	1	10	—	1808 April	20	By his Note	117	3	14	8
1807 April	29	To do	381			10							
Sept	24	To do	534		9								
Oct	22	To do	4		2								
Dec	12	To do	49		1	8							
	26	To do	57	1	4	8							
1808 Apl	20	To Interest	117		4	10							
				£ 5	12	—					£ 5	12	

Dr Charles Ledyard Cr

Date	Day	Particulars	Fol.	£	s	d	Date	Day	Particulars	Fol.	£	s	d
1805		To Ball: from page	16	1	17	4	1805 Octr	31	By his Note	249	5	14	2
Decr	13	To Merchandize &c	542	1	9	11							
1806 Jany	6	To do	8		1	1							
June	2	To do	106		2	2							
	5	To do	110	1	13	—							
	10	To do	119		5	3							
Octr	31	To Interest	249		5	5							
				£ 5	14	2					£ 5	14	2
1807 May	4	To Merchandize	385		6	—	1807 July	18	By Butter	467		6	—
1808 July	13	To Rye	179		7	—	1808 Aug	25	By Cash	256		7	—
1809 May	3	To Merchandize	345		6	8	1809 June	29	By Butter	331		7	11
June	19	To do	377		8	11	Sept	6	By Cash in full	422		10	5
July	3	To do	384		2	9							
				£ —	18	4					£ —	18	4

Dr Daniel Bowen Cr

Date	Day	Particulars	Fol.	£	s	d	Date	Day	Particulars	Fol.	£	s	d
1810 June	2	To Merchandize	22		1	9	1810 Novr	21	By Work	75	5	12	6
	8	To do	25		9	—							
	7	To Cash	27		9	9							
	11	To Cash	28	1	10	—							
	12	To Merchandize	30		4	6							
	25	To Sundries	38		6	9							
July	23	To Merchandize	51		7	9							
November	21	To Cash	75	2	3	—							
				£ 5	12	6					£ 5	12	6

You made your mon

and by gum, you o

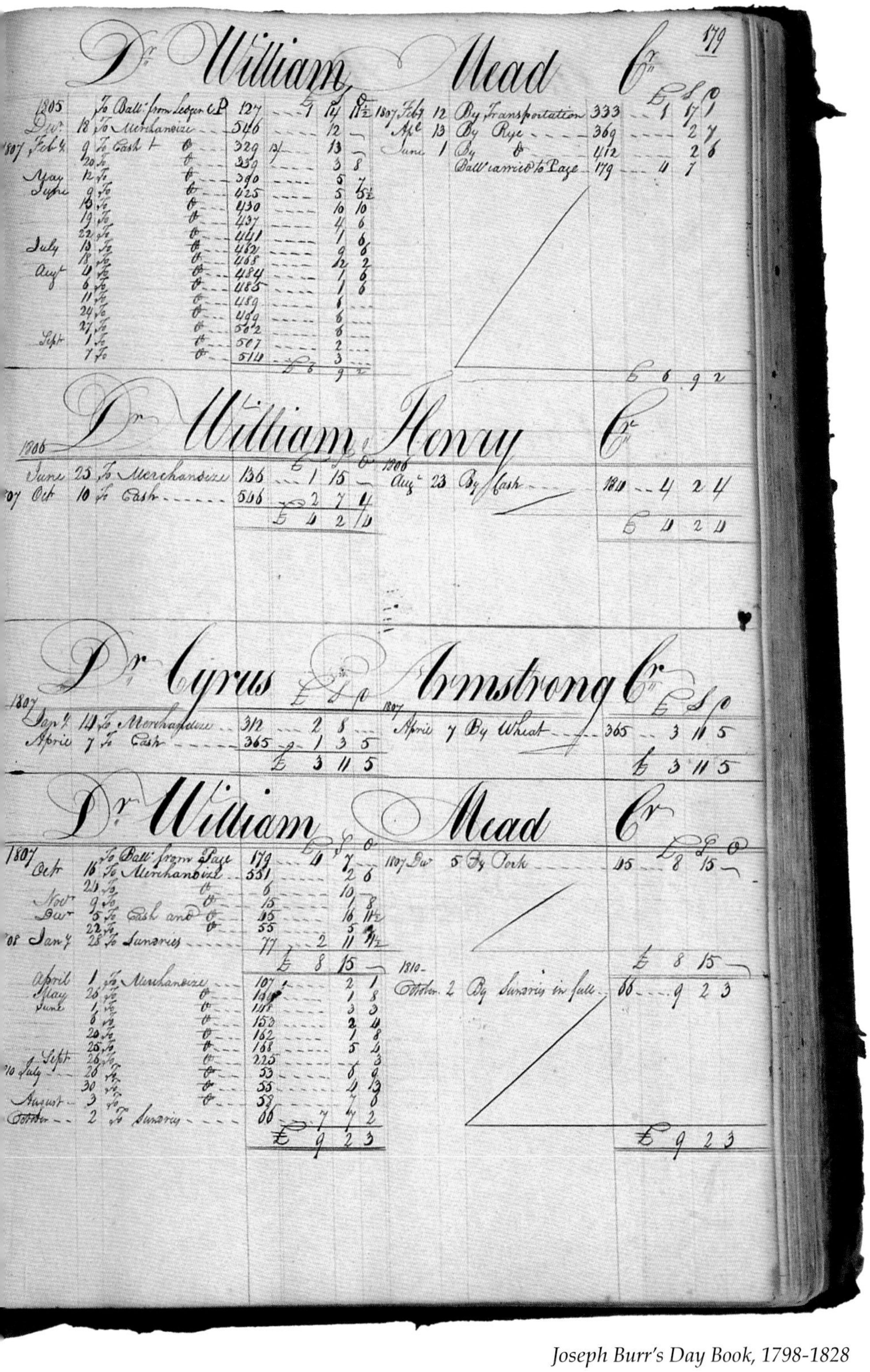

Joseph Burr's Day Book, 1798-1828

...ey off Vermonters,

...ght to leave it here.

Samuel Canfield of Arlington

In the name of God Amen I Joseph Burr of Manchester in
the County of Bennington & State of Vermont being in a weak
State of body but of sound & perfect mind & memory do make
ordain & publish this my last will & testament and devise
in manner & form following that is to say -
I give & bequeath to Lydia Black widow of Peter Black late of
said Manchester deceased my set of Scotts Bible, my sofa, my
bed & bedding in her possession, my bureau, two sets of Silver
table spoons & one set of Silver Tea spoons to be furnished by
my executors out of my estate -
I give & bequeath to Mariah Hitchcock, William P. Black,
James Black, Caroline Black children of said Peter Black and
to Lydia Ann Pratt wife of Jabesh Pratt, Sally Eliza Hitchcock
& Deborah Jane Hitchcock children of said Maria Hitchcock
to each one, the sum of One h
I give & bequeath to my Neph
Isaac Burr of the City of New
dollars -
I give & bequeath to Daniel Ki
neice Peggy C Kipsam of Nor
State of New York my watch a
-ship for him -
I also give & bequeath to the sa
of five thousand dollars in t
annual interest of the same
Kipsam Junr. & the other childr
-after be born of the said Dani
the said Children of the said Dan
a suitable education then the s
dollars hereby bequeathed to th
be divided equally among th

Joseph Burr's will, 1828

The gravesite of Joseph Burr and Josiah Burton in Dellwood Cemetery, Manchester Village

When Joseph Burr arrived in Manchester from Hempstead, Long Island, in 1793 he was just twenty years old. By the time he died thirty-five years later, this frontier merchant had amassed a fortune of $150,000. At a time when most men's assets were tied up in property, and bartering was still a widespread practice, Burr's accumulation of capital was a testament to his careful business practices and innate frugality.

The Manchester he knew was a small village on the edge of the colonial world. The oldest house was only thirty years old and the inhabitants numbered around 1,200. Situated on the crossroads of important New England trade routes, Manchester held promise for an ambitious entrepreneur, and so Burr made it his home, living and conducting his business in the heart of the village.

A lifelong bachelor, Burr was an educated man with a library of over 150 books. He tried politics, but gave it up as he could not bring himself to vote according to his constituents' desires. A frequent diner at Black's Tavern, the center of village social life, he knew everyone of consequence and they knew him. His daybook is filled with the names of Manchester's earliest citizens, many still recognizable after two centuries.

In the years before his death in 1828, several of his associates more than hinted that his substantial fortune ought to be used to found an academy in Manchester. The Reverend William Jackson, pastor of the Congregational Church in Dorset, is said to have been instrumental in convincing Burr of the wisdom of this proposal. But it was Samuel Canfield, patriarch of one of Arlington's most prominent families, who put it to him straight: "You made your money off Vermonters and by gum, you ought to leave it here."

In the end he took their advice. According to the provisions of his will, revised just weeks before his death, Burr bequeathed over two-thirds of his estate to education. In addition to funds for Williams, Dartmouth, and Middlebury colleges, he left $10,000 to found an academy in Manchester. But being the astute businessman he was, he added a challenging proviso – in order to secure the funds, the founders would have to match his bequest dollar for dollar within five years. The matching $10,000 was to be used for the construction and outfitting of the school. He made it clear that his original sum was to be held in perpetuity as an endowment, the interest from which was to be used as scholarship money to support "poor, needy, and pious youth preparatory to their entering theological studies."

The apparent seclusion of Manchester, in a picturesque valley, with fine mountain scenery and a healthy moral atmosphere, makes it a desirable place for the education of youth. The interest of its people in the establishment of Burr Seminary was evinced by their readiness to comply with the conditions of Mr. Burr's will, in erecting the necessary buildings, and their manifest pride in sustaining a school that should be an honor to the intelligence and resources of the town.

Elizabeth Wickham
wife of Joseph D. Wickham, the second principal

Elizabeth Merwin Wickham, born in Wilton, Connecticut, arrived with her husband, the Reverend Dr. Joseph D. Wickham and their daughter Emma, age three, in 1838. They had traveled up the Hudson River by barge and were met in Troy by a stage coach that took them to Manchester where Wickham was to become Burr Seminary's second and longest-serving principal.

of time upon what security and at what interest

All the power and authority given to the respective officers of the corporation are to be subject to and controled by the vote of the corporation at any regular meeting thereof – such vote having no effect upon any previous authorized act of any officer –

In witness whereof we have hereunto subscribed our names

Dated at Manchester aforesaid this 25th day of December AD 1831

Unlike many early academies, Burr Seminary was not founded by an itinerant teacher or a religious organization. The men who decided to accept Burr's challenge were Manchester's most distinguished community members – judges, lawyers, business owners, and even a former governor of Vermont. Erecting a school for higher education was a matter of civic pride to these men. It was also a matter of necessity to the community's other most prominent citizens, the Protestant clergymen. Religion was not a private matter in the founding years but was central to American life. Protestant denominations were an active civilizing force that strongly promoted education through several wide-ranging societies. Though it was certainly in their interest to educate young men to fill their own ranks, these highly educated men also clearly understood the fledgling democracy's need for an educated citizenry.

Richard Skinner
James Anderson.
John Aiken
Milo L. Bennett
Cyrus Munson
Wm Jackson.
John Whiton
Nathan Burton
Alexr Proudfit
Chs Walker
William Page.
John S. Pettibone
Joel Pratt
Nathan H. Bottum
Myron Clark

Additional Rules adopted by the Board at their Annual Meeting February AD 1832

"Resolved that in addition to and as a part of the Byla[ws] [o]f this Corporation, there shall be appointed & Elected at [t]he time & in the manner and for the same Term as th[e] their regular officers of the Corporation a Committee [c]onsisting of three members of the Corporation, denomi[n]ated the Executive Committee, whose duty it sha[ll b]e in conjunction with the principal instructor to [e]xamine & admit or reject all such poor needy & pious you[ng]

In an 1860 address to Burr Seminary graduates, Reverend James Anderson, an original trustee and friend of Burr's, revealed that Burr was not optimistic that his friends would be able to raise the money. It was a large sum for a small outpost – approximately twenty times a teacher's annual salary in the 1820s. Nevertheless, the three men named in his will, John Aiken, an attorney, Myron Clark, and Cyrus Munson, went forward with the articles of incorporation the following year. Taking the first step toward raising money proved to be more difficult. In 1830, though it was hard work, they did manage to come up with the $10,000, over $7,000 of which was raised in Manchester. The balance came from several of the education societies and from generous donors from other parts of the state. In 1831 the trustees voted to proceed with construction.

Burr Seminary was the first secondary school to be incorporated by the Vermont State Legislature and is the oldest continuously operating secondary school in Vermont. It is also one of less than a dozen New England academies still in existence.

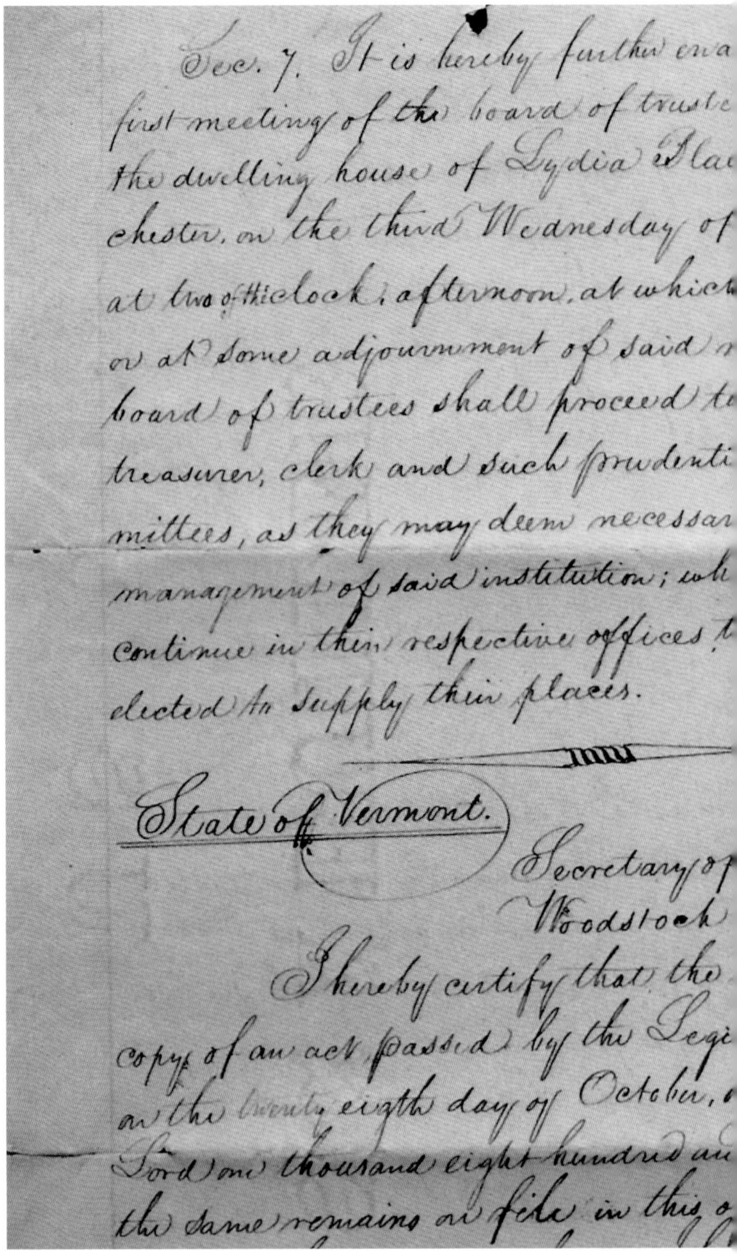

I find the only way to m
at all is to go to their do
them.... I find it is very
only way is to take it pa

...d, That the
be holden at
in said Man-
December next
time and place,
...ting, the said
...lect a president.
or other standing com-
for the proper
officers shall
others are duly

State's Office.
Nov. 20. 1829.
...egoing is a true
...ture of this state;
the year of our
twenty nine, ...
...ice.

An Act establishing an Academy at Manchester in the county of Bennington.

Whereas Joseph Burr, late of Manchester in the county of Bennington, deceased, by his last will and testament, bequeathed the sum of ten thousand dollars, as a permanent fund for the promotion of education in the village of said Manchester, where he the said Joseph had resided, and by his said will provided that the said fund might be paid over to a corporation or the treasurer thereof, which might be established, for the purpose of promoting such education in said village, within five years from the time of his decease: — To the end, therefore of carrying into effect the public and charitable intentions of the said donor, and of such others as may choose to patronise the cause of learning and piety:

Sec. 1. It is hereby enacted by the General As...

Articles of Incorporation, 1829

*ake people do anything
ors and hammer it into
slow hard work but the
tiently and perservere.*

Letter from C. Shumway to the trustees, March 1831

Invoice for building materials, 1832

Your committee beg leave to add that they have deeply felt and regretted that the expenses incurred so far exceeds their own expectations and those of the board and that it has not been in their power to inform the board from time to time as to the exact amount of expenditures and probable expenses. They trust they have already given a satisfactory explanation of the unpropitious events which have led inevitably to these difficulties. Their contracts have been defeated and their plans thwarted by events not under control and which no foresight of theirs could either have anticipated or prevented.

Trustees Building Committee, 1832

The land for the new school, forty acres on the west side of the village, was given to the trustees by two local families, the Munsons and the Blacks. Ephraim Munson sold the trustees the right to bring water over his property for a small price. The locals called the new school "the castle in the pasture."

Seminary Building, 1872

The trustees' difficulties were not confined to raising the money. Seminary Building was originally designed to be built of brick. Over 180,000 bricks had been burned in Mr. Goodale's kiln before it was discovered that something had gone terribly wrong. The bricks crumbled in the workmen's hands and were declared unfit for use. The trustees were faced with a terrible dilemma. To wait for more bricks to be made would have meant missing the deadline specified in Burr's will and forfeiting his bequest. What else could they use for exterior building materials? Fortunately, a successful limestone quarry had recently opened behind the school on Mt. Equinox.

Stonemasons quickly replaced bricklayers as the race to finish the building began. The trustees made it by the skin of their teeth. In November 1832, four months before the expiration date stipulated in Burr's will, Seminary Building was appraised for $11,250 and Burr's bequest secured. When it was completed, it was one of the largest buildings in Vermont.

Their success was clouded by the fact that the building had cost $4,250 more than they had anticipated. Seriously in debt before the doors had even opened, the trustees vowed to move ahead. Unfinished work on the interior pushed the opening date from December to the following May. The choice of brick and then stone, in a region where the majority of buildings were built of wood, is a strong indication of how the founders conceived of the 16,000-square-foot, four-story building to be an important and permanent institution.

Seminary was a word commonly used in the nineteenth century to describe a college preparatory school. Though Mr. Burr did leave a permanent fund of $10,000 to provide scholarships for "needy and pious youth" wishing to study for the ministry, the majority of students did not enroll for this purpose.

Students on application for admission to be examined as to moral character & general conduct as well as scholarship. No scholar of bad character to be received or retained.

Reverend Joseph Anderson
Plan for Conducting the Seminary

Success will depend upon character of instruction and discipline. . . .

Burr Seminary Catalog, 1836

In planning the school's structure, the founding trustees had the idea that a working farm and a machine shop would provide income to the school through student labor. They went to the considerable trouble and expense of building a waterwheel as a source of energy for the expensive machinery they thought to instruct the students to use. Unfortunately, this novel idea proved too costly to the young school that seemed ever to be struggling for funds and it was quickly abandoned.

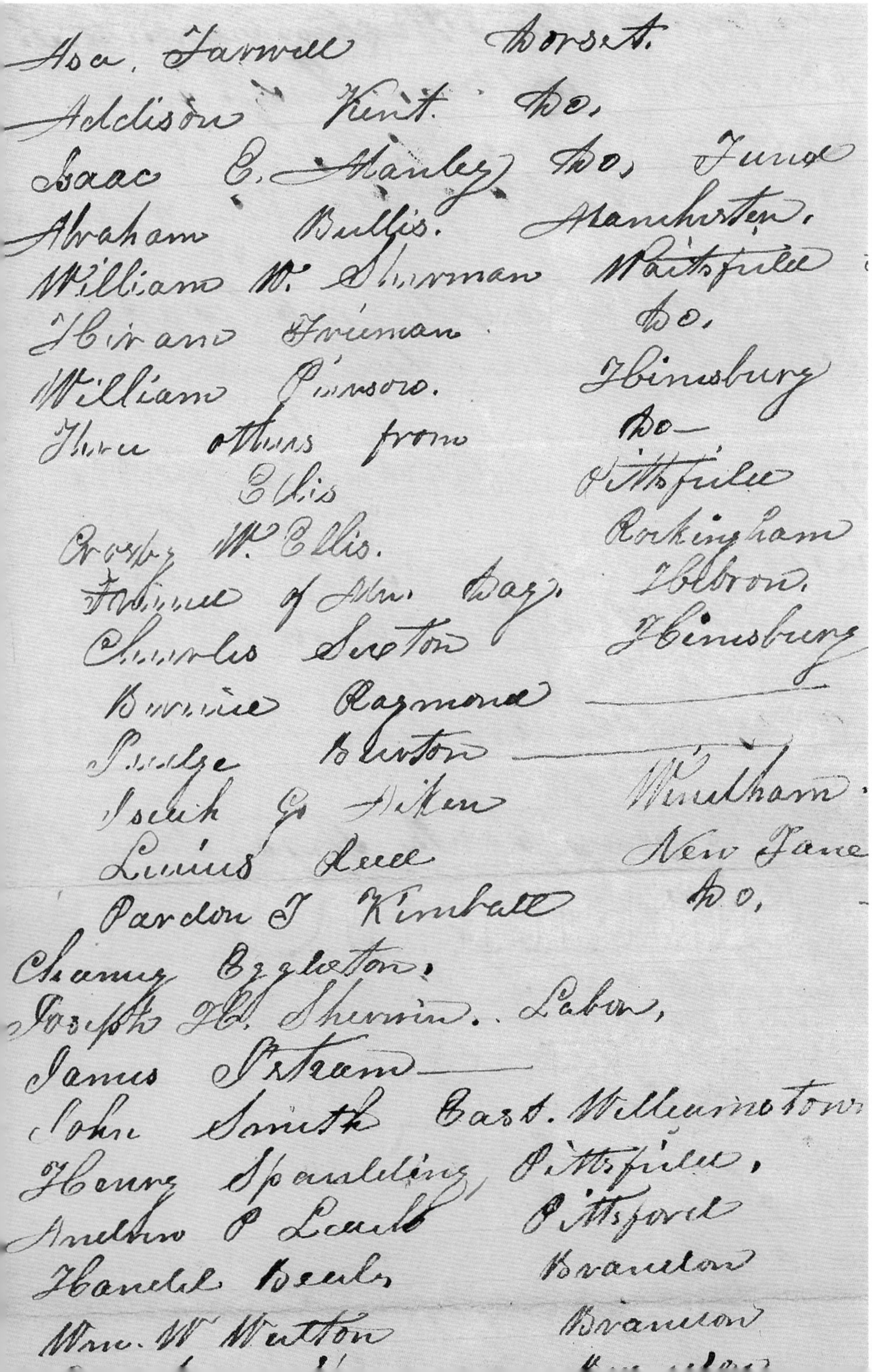
Asa. Farwell Dorset.
Addison Kent. Do.
Isaac C. Hanley Do. June
Abraham Bullis. Manchester.
William W. Sherman Waitsfield
Hiram Freeman. Do.
William Pinson. Kinsbury
Three others from Do
Ellis Pittsfield
Crosby W. Ellis. Rockingham
Friend of Mr. Day. Albion.
Charles Sexton Kinsbury
Bruce Raymond
Dudge Burton
Isaiah G. Allen Windham.
Lucius Reed New Fane
Pardon T. Kimball Do.
Chauncy Eggleston.
Joseph H. Sherwin. Labor,
James Ostram
John Smith East Williamstown
Henry Spaulding Pittsfield,
Andrew P. Leach Pittsford
Handel Beeles Brandon
Wm. W. Wetton Brandon

As there were no laws at the time regarding how old an applicant must be, the students ranged in age from twelve to eighteen. The only prerequisite was ability to do the work, a good character, and willingness to follow the rules.

If I am not mistaken, I was the first boy entered at the Seminary.

Thomas Canfield

Thomas Canfield, son of Samuel Canfield, was among the first students to attend Burr Seminary. He later became president of the Northern Pacific Railroad.

STUDENTS.

CLASSICAL DEPARTMENT.

NAMES.	RESIDENCE.	ROOMS.
George Alden,	*Orwell,*	No. 30.
George W. Ash,	*Putney,*	No. 17.
Gamaliel I. Baker,	*Fort Ann, N. Y.,*	No. 22.
A. Z. Bardin,	*Dalton, Mass.,*	No. 16.
Edmund H. Bennett,	*Manchester,*	Mr. M. L. Bennett's.
John C. Briggs,	*Manchester,*	Mr. Briggs'.
Joseph D. Briggs,	*Manchester,*	Mr. Briggs'.
Josephus Brockway,	*Troy, N. Y.,*	Mr. B. Munson's.
Joseph Brooks,	*Halifax,*	No. 14.
Thomas H. Canfield,	*Arlington,*	Mr. B. Munson's.
E. S. Capron,	*Hoosick, N. Y.,*	No. 9.
Charles Churchill,	*Moores, N. Y.,*	Mr. Watson's.
John A. Collins,	*Manchester,*	Mrs. Collins'.
John N. Cramer,	*Granville, N. Y.,*	No. 25.
Samuel H. Cross,	*Corinth,*	No. 14.
Lewis Curtiss,	*Dorset,*	No. 7.
John Curtiss,	*Dorset,*	No. 7.
C. Minot Davey,	*Fair Haven,*	No. 17.
Joel S. Everitt,	*Halifax,*	No. 19.
Asahel C. Geer,	*Glen's Falls, N. Y.,*	Mr. Coleman's.
Nelson Gray,	*Dorset,*	No. 15.
James T. Hamlin,	*Moreau, N. Y.,*	Mr. B. Munson's.
David B. Hall,	*Granville, N. Y.,*	No. 25.
Fletcher J. Hawley,	*Arlington,*	Mr. B. Munson's.
John Hitchcock,	*Pittsford,*	No. 16.
Edward Hollister,	*Connewango, N. Y.,*	No. 23.
James Hopkins,	*Hebron, N. Y.,*	No. 15.
Charles A. Huntington,	*St. Albans,*	No. 26.
John Isham,	*Manchester,*	Mrs. Isham's.
J. Sumner Kidder,	*Alstead, N. H.,*	No. 25.
Samuel Kidder,	*Wardsboro,*	No. 12.
Edward King,	*Burlington,*	No. 23.

2

The doors opened to 114 young men on May 15, 1833. The Reverend Lyman Coleman, a Yale College graduate, was first principal (so-called because he was the principal teacher). As the trustees had taken care to advertise widely, students came from all over New England. The opening fortuitously coincided with a wave of religious revivalism. The offer of free tuition and board for those contemplating the ministry attracted many young men of maturity and sobriety thus setting the tone in the early years.

The purpose of the school being the preparation of young men for college, the curriculum for the Classical Department met the requirements considered essential by the handful of institutions of higher learning then in existence. The three-year course, consisting of readings in Latin and Greek, changed very little during the entire nineteenth century.

The Reverend Joseph D. Wickham

Elizabeth Merwin Wickham

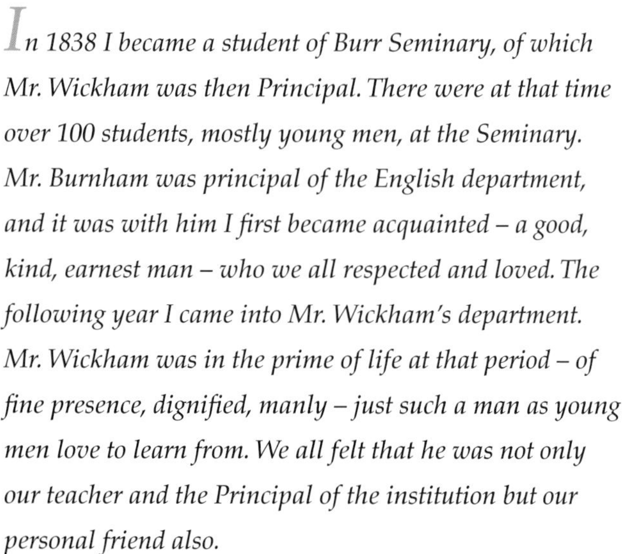
In 1838 I became a student of Burr Seminary, of which Mr. Wickham was then Principal. There were at that time over 100 students, mostly young men, at the Seminary. Mr. Burnham was principal of the English department, and it was with him I first became acquainted – a good, kind, earnest man – who we all respected and loved. The following year I came into Mr. Wickham's department. Mr. Wickham was in the prime of life at that period – of fine presence, dignified, manly – just such a man as young men love to learn from. We all felt that he was not only our teacher and the Principal of the institution but our personal friend also.

Dr. W. E. Merriman, Class of 1840

Mr. Anderson in the afternoon harnessed up Jack and took us on to Seminary Hill to view our future home – which eventually proved to be one for 25 years. It was vacation so the school was not in session. We went into the dining room of the Seminary and met there Mrs. M[erriman], the kindly wife of the steward. . . . Mr. M[erriman] soon came in and took us into the brick house which looked pleasant and convenient tho now new. . . . The brick house which was to be our home was well built and convenient – a pleasant home to us for over 20 years. The Burr Seminary was commodious but the money appropriated to it had been given out before it was fairly completed – so nice furnishings were out of the question – there being no paint on the doors or window frames of the students rooms nor any closets. But all were furnished with strong box stoves so that there was no lack of comfort. The high basement was convenient for the boarding department and the large north apartment on the first floor called the chapel was a pleasant gathering place for the pupils of the school.

Elizabeth Wickham

The Reverend Joseph Anderson

The original First Congregational Church (left) in Manchester Village

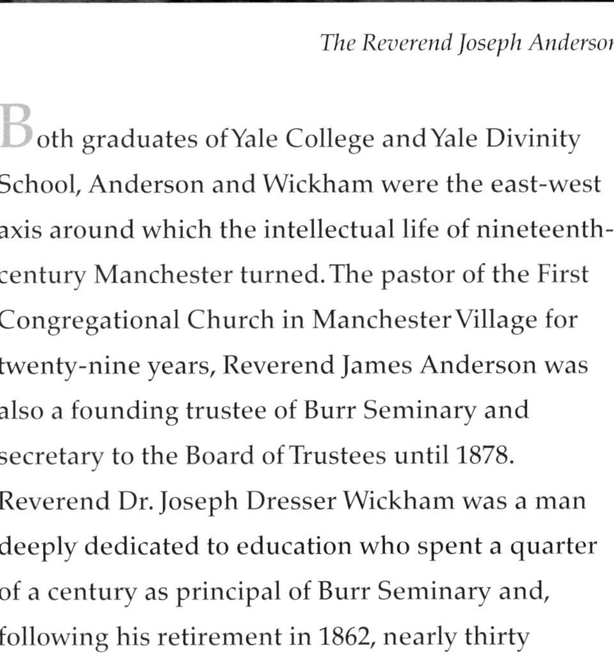

Both graduates of Yale College and Yale Divinity School, Anderson and Wickham were the east-west axis around which the intellectual life of nineteenth-century Manchester turned. The pastor of the First Congregational Church in Manchester Village for twenty-nine years, Reverend James Anderson was also a founding trustee of Burr Seminary and secretary to the Board of Trustees until 1878. Reverend Dr. Joseph Dresser Wickham was a man deeply dedicated to education who spent a quarter of a century as principal of Burr Seminary and, following his retirement in 1862, nearly thirty years a president of its Board of Trustees.

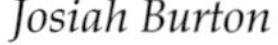
Josiah Burton

William Burnham

In 1849, sixteen young women entered Burr Seminary on a trial basis. They called themselves the "Forty-Niners." The girls who wanted to study Greek and Latin just like the boys at Burr Seminary had a champion in William Burnham, the head of the English Department, whose own young daughters were among the agitators. In colonial times, women had not been denied an education beyond the elementary level; higher education simply was not considered necessary. And until the founding of Mt. Holyoke in 1837, there wasn't even a college for them to aspire to attend. All this was changing in the 1840s. Just 200 miles to the west in Seneca, New York, the first women's rights convention had taken place in July 1848.

Josiah Burton, one of the founding trustees and another prosperous bachelor, had witnessed within his own extended family the determination of young women to pursue higher education. When Burton died in 1855, he left $6,000 for the establishment of a female seminary in Manchester if certain conditions could be met within five years. If not, the funds would be given to his fellow trustees for the same purpose. Though there is evidence in the Board's minutes that the trustees contemplated erecting a building for young women on school grounds, in the end they made provision for separate rooms within Seminary Building. In 1860, the school's original charter was amended to record the new name chosen by the trustees to honor their benefactor: Burr and Burton Seminary. That same year, sixty-seven of the 199 students enrolled were young women.

Emma Wickham Roe, Class of 1852

Lucy Barrett, Class of 1849

Wishing to pursue some branches of study to finish her preparation for entering Mt. Holyoke Seminary, Miss Barrett applied to Mr. William Burnham, Assistant Principal, for private instruction. Mr. Burnham replied he had not the time, and thinking for a moment said, "Why not come to the Seminary, and join the classes in those branches?" She did so and was soon followed by Frances Walker, Emma Wickham, myself and others.

There were no green campus and fine trees to greet the eye. The hill was bleak and bare, no marble sidewalk, the students walked in the road. There was a rough board fence and a large gate, and a flight of steps each side of the fence, very near the late Mr. Coy's shoe store, across the Avenue. In the winter, walking through the deep snow was laborious. I was provided with a pair of men's boots. I remember they had very pointed toes. I was at once called Puss in Boots and a handsome black-eyed, rosy-cheeked lad was daily on watch for Puss, to take her books as he held the door open.

Caroline Anderson recalling her experience as a Forty-Niner, 1890

Samuel Burnham, Class of 1855

I wish these difficulties could be settled in some way honorable to us; it seems as if blood enough had been spilled already. The battle of Sharpsburg was the most bloody one of the war. I have seen the dead piled up at Fair Oaks, Savage Station, White Oak Swamp, Bull Run, and many other places but never saw such slaughter as our troops made among the rebels on the 17th.

Letter from Lieut. Samuel Burnham,
Hagerstown, Maryland
October 7, 1862

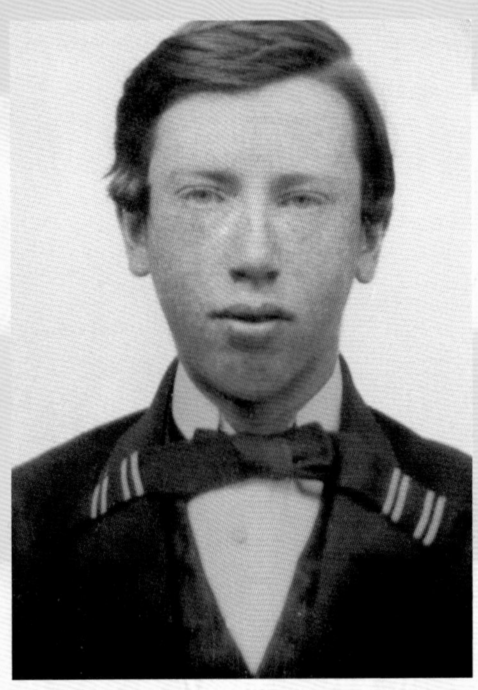

Cyrus Hard, Class of 1861

At Vienna we were drawn up in a line in a pasture and stood there till dark. We couldn't see far it was so foggy. There were lines of something that looked like cavalry but it might have been nothing but a fence. Our cavalry and skirmishers went on and did not come in till dark. I do not know if they saw anything or not. We marched six miles and back through the mud and rain without stopping to rest coming back and were not near as tired as on the other march. We did not have to carry our knapsacks. All that troubled us was that we did not have a chance to see any rebels and couldn't get any prisoners or plunder.

Letter from Cyrus Hard
November 10, 1861

Despite being severely wounded, Isaac Burton '61 grabbed his fallen regimental flag from the battlefield at Savage Station and carried it to safety.

Class of 1880

1866	First reunion of old students is held in Manchester
1874	First alumni association is formed
1875	Tradition of Senior Class Day established
1885	Steam heat and running water are installed in Seminary Building
1891	Reverend Joseph D. Wickham, president of the Board of Trustees, dies on May 15

II *Thoroughness & Permanence*

1864 - 1891

This drawing of the school buildings appeared as an advertisement in the 1870s.

Seminary Building in the early 1870s

The town has long been noted for the intelligence, culture and high-toned character of its people and its freedom from the usual temptations to vice found in most places of its size. The people take a deep interest in the success of the school.

Catalog, 1878

In the years immediately following the Civil War, Burr and Burton continued to thrive despite a series of principals who left after a short time and some financial worries that the Board of Trustees continued to address. The expense of operating the school had increased substantially. To keep the school going, the trustees borrowed judiciously and Dr. Wickham contacted alumni who were willing to make generous donations. Enrollment, never over 150 before the war, went from a high of 224 in 1868 to a low of eighty-eight in 1879.

Rules and Regulations.

REQUIREMENTS.

1. Prompt attendance at Daily Prayers, Church and Bible Service on the Sabbath, as well as a careful observance of the day.
2. Hours of study and rest to be strictly kept.
3. All rooms to be put in order before the ringing of the breakfast bell, and to be kept clean and neat at all times.
4. Careful use of rooms and all Seminary furniture.
5. Promptness in all the exercises of the school.
6. All lights to be extinguished and all students to retire by 10 P.M.
7. Payment of all damage to room or Seminary property.
8. Gentlemanly and lady-like deportment towards students, teachers and citizens at all times.

PROHIBITIONS.

1. Visiting Ladies' Hall or Rooms without permission.
2. Persons not members of the Seminary visiting students' rooms without permission.
3. Absence from, or noise in rooms during hours of study or rest.
4. Removing furniture or bedding from one room to another.
5. Absence from the Seminary after the ringing of the evening bell, or on the Sabbath.
6. Writing upon the walls or defacing any Seminary property.
7. Loud talking or laughing, scuffling or running in halls or rooms at any time.

Catalog, 1877

By 1873 it was clear that extensive repairs were again necessary. "It was in the course of the repairs now undertaken that the first change was made affecting the outward appearance of the old building. The small lighted windows of the original structure were replaced by those now in use. It was at this time also that the benches in the north chapel, well worn from their forty years service, were retired."

The arrival of W. H. Shaw as principal in 1872 lifted spirits as he was well-educated, young, and dedicated. During his six years as the head of school, he brought a renewed energy and instituted many changes, beginning with the rules and regulations. During the 1870s, several innovative traditions were instituted at Burr and Burton. Graduates received diplomas for the first time in 1870, and in 1871 students began to receive regular report cards. The first issue of *The Seminary Courant* in June 1875 contains an article describing the establishment of Senior Class Day and the planting of the first-class tree which would remain school traditions for seventy-five years.

Prohibitions initiated by Principal Shaw included the first mention of baseball: "All games of chance, the use of gunpowder in or around the Seminary building, the use of intoxicating drinks, profane or indecent language, smoking at any time or place, loitering around hotels, stores, post-office, or any place of resort, playing ball with associations or persons not members of the Seminary, or leaving town for any cause." There were several baseball associations in town during these years but as yet no organized athletic teams at the school.

Charles Orvis, Class of 1851

Franklin Orvis (right) attended Burr Seminary in the late 1830s.

Mr. Franklin Orvis, the founder and proprietor of the Equinox House . . . was by nature a sociable authoritarian old English squire. He had a brother, a diminutive being, a fiery Democrat, highly intelligent and very well informed – every half inch a man. The verbal battles of the two made village history. Orvis Cottage, where Mr. Charles Orvis lived, was only a few doors north of the Equinox, and on all high holidays, when the great flag was hung across the street between the Equinox office and the court-house, Mr. Charles Orvis hung one of equal size across the street between the Orvis Cottage and the engine house. In election years, the Equinox flag bore the names of the Republican nominees in large print across the bottom. The Orvis Cottage flag in like manner bore the names of the Democratic nominees.

In Cleveland's terms, Mr. Charles Orvis was the postmaster; and the children of the town, indeed the grown-ups too, were apt to tip-toe when they entered the post office. In winter we very carefully and earnestly shut the door. I once heard Mr. Orvis, standing five feet erect in his tiny shoes, tell big John Wild that if he left that door open again, he would find himself flat on his back in the middle of the street.

It was this dragon postmaster who qualified, to my mind at least, as the most gallant lover in Manchester. It was said that for all his irascible nature, he had never said one cross word to his serene, gentle old wife. He survived her about ten years; and on every Sunday afternoon in spring, summer, and fall, we saw him pass our house going down to the cemetery with flowers for her grave.

Sarah Cleghorn, Class of 1895
from her memoirs *Threescore*

Mary Orvis Marbury, Class of 1872

Charles's daughter Mary Orvis Marbury '72, helped her father to run his fishing tackle business. Her 1892 book, *Favorite Flies and Their Histories*, a long treatise on flies and fly tying, won acclaim at the 1893 World's Columbian Exposition in Chicago and has become a collector's item.

Local alumni were establishing themselves as prominent leaders in the community. As successful businessmen, they contributed greatly to the prosperity of Manchester and none more successfully at this time than the Orvis brothers.

The Orvis family were early and consistent supporters of the school. Levi Orvis, who owned a popular store in Manchester Village, was one of the original subscribers, contributing $100 to the Burr challenge. His sons Charles, Franklin, and Levi all attended Burr Seminary, and daughter Caroline was the first preceptress for girls in 1849.

In 1853, Franklin Orvis bought the home his father had built on Main Street in 1832, enlarged it, and opened Equinox House. The hotel soon made a name for itself as a first-class resort, and counted among its early guests Mrs. Abraham Lincoln and her son Robert in 1861. Franklin graciously hosted the many Burr and Burton reunions held in the late nineteenth century which attracted several hundred alumni. A far-sighted real estate developer as well, Franklin bought numerous lots in the village that were later successfully developed. In 1865 he deeded land to his alma mater at no cost.

Originally the village surgeon-dentist, Charles Orvis later founded the Orvis Company next door to his brother's business in 1856. The company's reputation and appeal to fly-fishing aficionados earned it an international following that brought many visitors to Manchester. Members of the Orvis family would continue to attend Burr and Burton and run both the Equinox House and the Orvis Company until well into the twentieth century.

D. K. Simonds

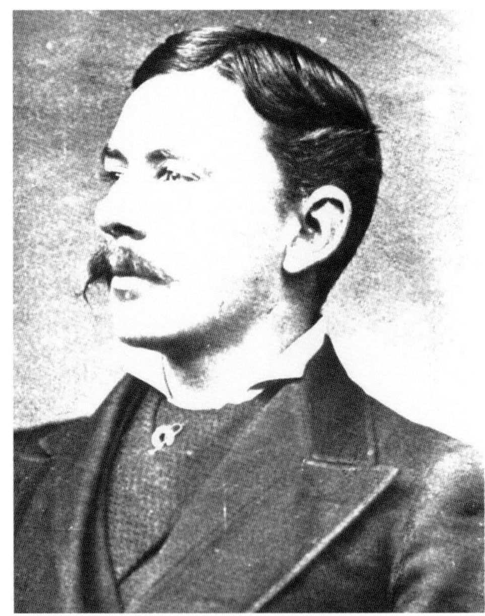

Joseph Wickham Fowler

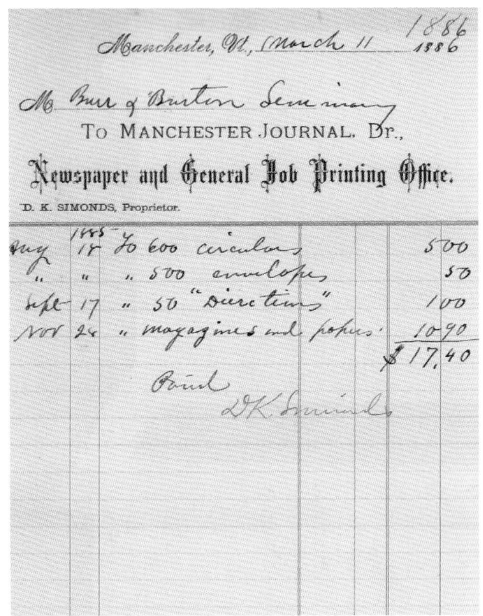

Manchester, Vt., March 11 1886

M Burr & Burton Seminary

TO MANCHESTER JOURNAL, Dr.,

Newspaper and General Job Printing Office.

D. K. SIMONDS, Proprietor.

	1885		
Aug	18	To 600 circulars	5 00
"	"	" 500 envelopes	50
Sept	17	" 50 "Directions"	1 00
Nov	24	" magazines and papers	10 90
			$17.40

Paid

D K Simonds

The Manchester Journal *was founded in 1861*

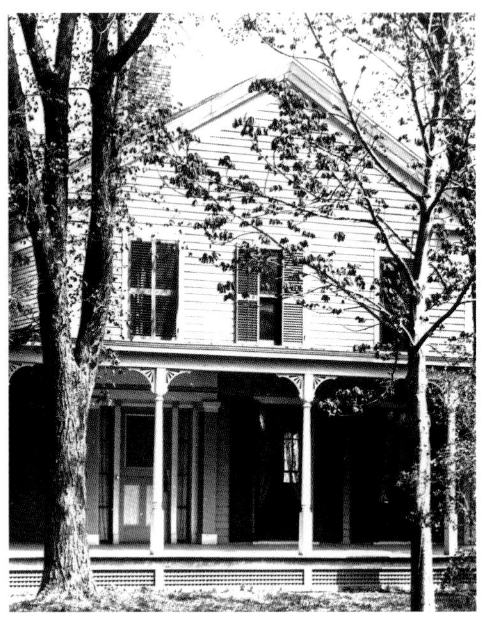

Fowler Insurance Company, 1890s

A member of the class of 1859, David Kendall Simonds was an active citizen of Manchester for over fifty years. Following his graduation from Middlebury and service with the Union Army, Simonds returned to Manchester to become editor of the *Manchester Journal*. In 1871, he bought the newspaper from Franklin Orvis and began a long and influential career as editor. Simonds was also the Village postmaster in the 1870s, town clerk from 1873-1908, and clerk of the Burr and Burton Board of Trustees from 1887 until his death in 1917. In 1905 Simonds sold the *Journal* to another Burr and Burton alumnus, Otto Bennett '84.

The Hon. H. K. Fowler '40 arrived in Manchester as a young man from Poughkeepsie, New York. He entered Burr Seminary and following graduation he studied law. In addition to being a leading lawyer in town, he began the first insurance company in Manchester. His eldest son, who would continue the insurance business, was named Joseph Wickham Fowler after his good friend and mentor, the principal of Burr Seminary. The Fowler Insurance Company would continue to be operated by family members until it merged with Briggs Insurance to become the present-day Briggs-Fowler Insurance Company. All subsequent generations of the Fowler family continued to attend Burr and Burton.

In 1879, John Heinel, a tailor, opened Heinel's Clothing Store on Main Street. His son, Frederick H. Heinel '00, continued the business and served as a trustee of the school in the 1930s. Frederick P. Heinel '31 inherited the family business and oversaw its move to its current location in 1972. Heinel family members continued to attend Burr and Burton and to run the family business for over 100 years until its sale.

James Black '52 was a founder and the first head cashier at Factory Point National Bank which was organized in 1883. The great-grandson of Peter Black, who kept the tavern where Joseph Burr dined, James continued a family tradition in banking. His grandfather, William A. Black, had been town clerk, town treasurer, and cashier of the first Manchester Bank as well as its later incarnations, the Battenkill Bank and the Battenkill National Bank. His father William P. Black, also a banker, was treasurer of the Burr and Burton Board of Trustees from 1842 until his death in 1887.

John C. Heinel

James P. Black

Heinel's Clothing Store and the Factory Point Bank were for many years in the same building on Main Street.

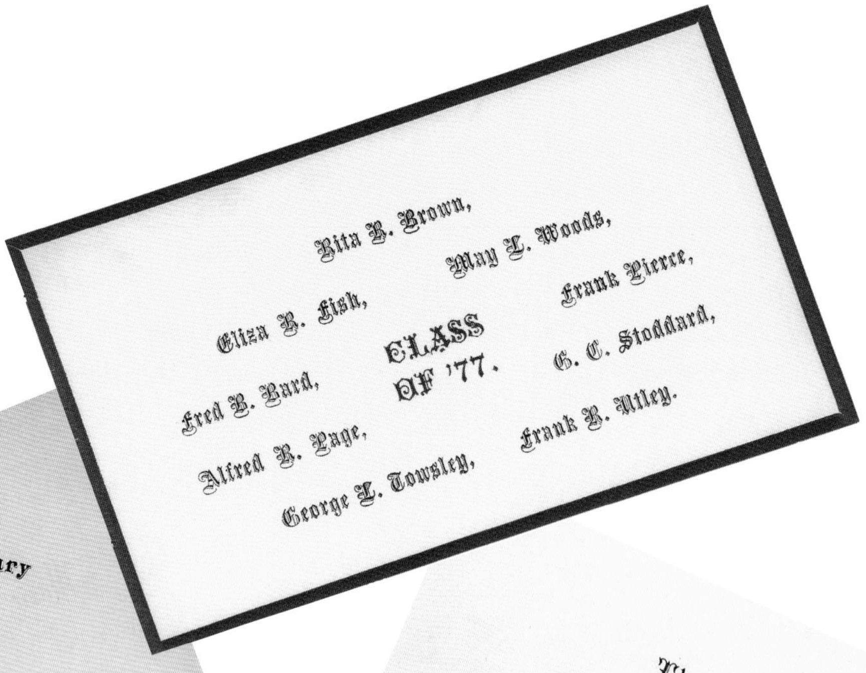

Rita B. Brown,
May L. Woods,
Eliza B. Fish,
Frank Pierce,
CLASS OF '77.
Fred B. Bard,
G. C. Stoddard,
Alfred B. Page,
Frank B. Wiley.
George L. Towsley,

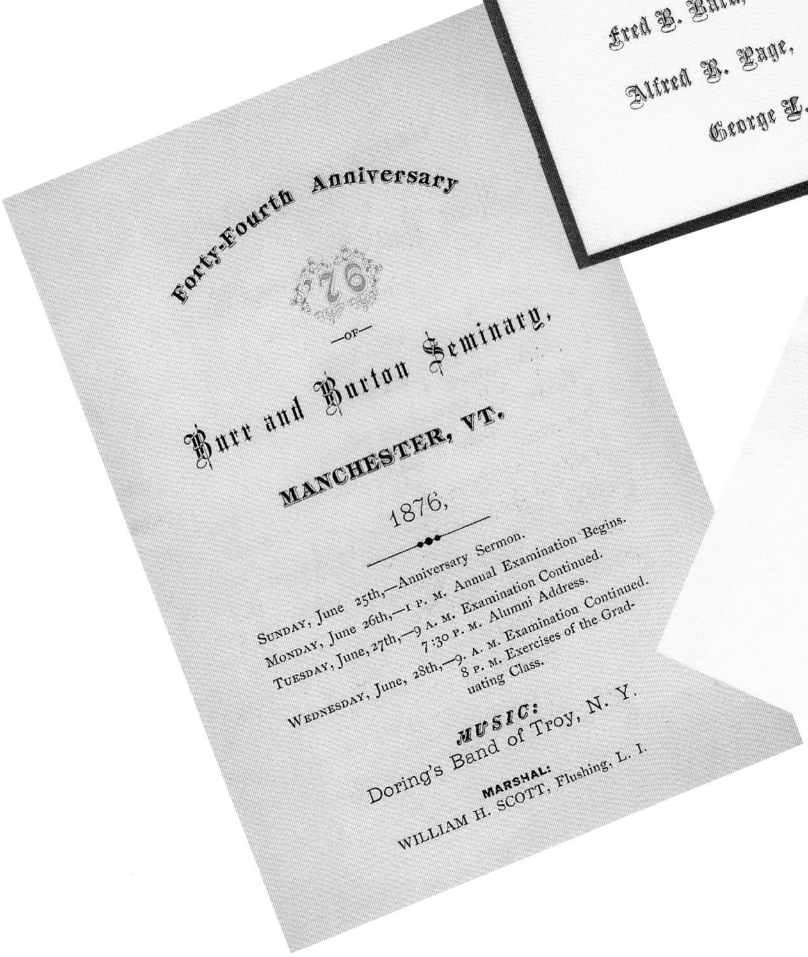

Forty-Fourth Anniversary

'76

—OF—

Burr and Burton Seminary,

MANCHESTER, VT.

1876,

SUNDAY, June 25th,—Anniversary Sermon.
MONDAY, June 26th,—1 P. M. Annual Examination Begins.
TUESDAY, June, 27th,—9 A. M. Examination Continued.
7:30 P. M. Alumni Address.
WEDNESDAY, June, 28th,—9. A. M. Examination Continued.
8 P. M. Exercises of the Graduating Class.

MUSIC:
Doring's Band of Troy, N. Y.

MARSHAL:
WILLIAM H. SCOTT, Flushing, L. I.

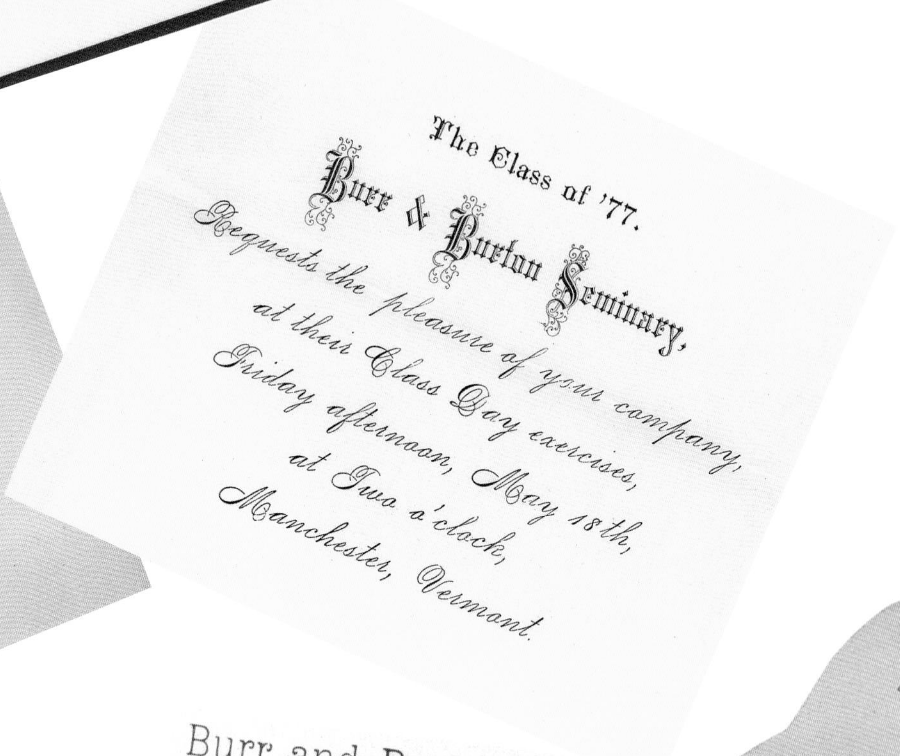

The Class of '77.
Burr & Burton Seminary,
Requests the pleasure of your company,
at their Class Day exercises,
Friday afternoon, May 18th,
at Two o'clock,
Manchester, Vermont.

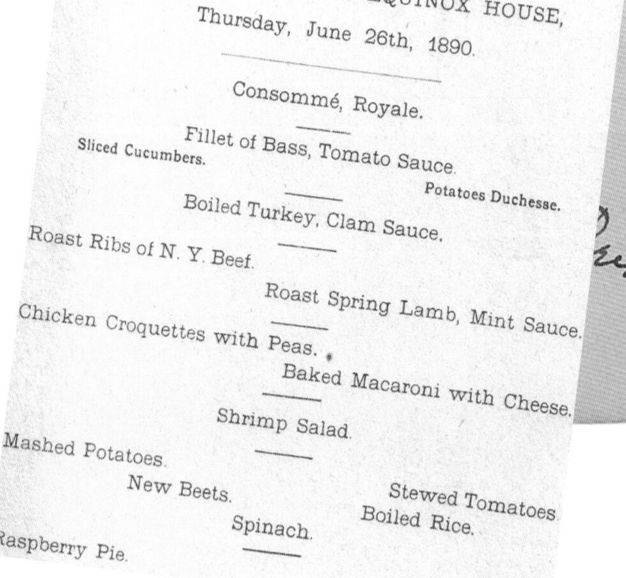

Burr and Burton Seminary.

REUNION, 1890.

ALUMNI DINNER AT EQUINOX HOUSE,
Thursday, June 26th, 1890.

Consommé, Royale.

Fillet of Bass, Tomato Sauce.
Sliced Cucumbers.
Potatoes Duchesse.

Boiled Turkey, Clam Sauce.

Roast Ribs of N. Y. Beef.
Roast Spring Lamb, Mint Sauce.
Chicken Croquettes with Peas.
Baked Macaroni with Cheese.

Shrimp Salad.

Mashed Potatoes.
New Beets.
Stewed Tomatoes.
Boiled Rice.
Spinach.

Raspberry Pie.
Custard Pie.

I hear again the Seminary bell. I am standing again in its classrooms. I am rolling pumpkins up and down its long upper hallway. I am "speaking my piece" in the boys' chapel, which to my excited imagination, I recall even yet as the largest stage I have ever seen. I am tugging and pulling at Reulo's horse power, the elevation of which to a roof top nearly lost me my diploma.

Charles H. Burritt, Class of 1871

Two courses of study continued to be offered, English and Classical, "which fits young men for any of our New England colleges and for teachers." The school year was divided into three terms, and tuition, room, and board was set at $70 per term. Day scholars were charged $8 per term for the Classical course and $6 for the English course. Extra courses were offered in Chemistry, French, and German, as well as drawing and oil painting.

Many members of the Manchester Cornet Band that marched the Equinox Guards off to the Civil War in September 1861 were Burr and Burton students and alumni. The group was forced to disband shortly thereafter as many of its members went off to join the Union Army.

The study of music in the late 1800s was very serious at Burr and Burton. In 1874, Mrs. D. K. Simonds became the music teacher and established the first music department. A graduate of the New England Conservatory of Music, she created an extensive curriculum which she continued to offer during the twenty-two years she taught at Burr and Burton. Students were offered five levels or "grades" through which they could progress from Foundation Studies by Emery to Beethoven's *Sonatas*. Three grades were offered in vocal instruction and students could also take courses in musical composition.

THE OPERETTA

FAIRY GROTTO.

Under the Direction of Mrs. D. K. SIMONDS.

Friday Evening August 26th, '81

AT MUSIC HALL, MANCHESTER,

Admission 25 Cts. Reserved Seats 50 Cts.

For Sale at the Usual Places.

Proceeds to be Devoted to Purchasing a Cabinet Organ for Burr and Burton Seminary.

Doors Open at 7 O'clock. Commences Promptly at 8.

Mrs. D. K. Simonds, music teacher

Class of 1888

It was founded in the prayers and hopes of the people, and its long array of honored names among its graduates shows the high rank it has taken among sister institutions, as well as the wisdom of its founders.

Circular, 1882

In the early years, students and faculty marked the end of the school year with Anniversary Exercises at the Congregational Church. The day-long program would include declamations, recitations, and an address by a visiting clergyman. By the 1880s, graduation had taken on the characteristics more familiar to later generations. Invitations were sent and on the appointed day students, parents, and faculty would gather at the Music Hall in the Village. A formal portrait of the graduates also marked the occasion.

Class of 1889

Milton Severance '59 and a graduate of Middlebury College, became the first alumnus to serve as principal (1882-1887). Many early graduates went on to have distinguished careers: Lewis Grout '38 compiled the first grammar of the Zulu language; Lyman Knapp '58 was elected governor of Alaska in 1889; Arthur Canfield '73 became a distinguished professor at the University of Michigan; and William Wickham '50 was mayor of New York City in the 1870s.

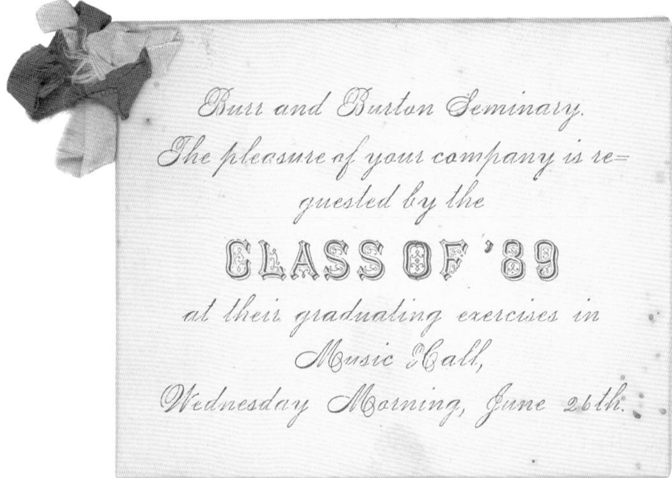

Burr and Burton Seminary.
The pleasure of your company is re-
quested by the
CLASS OF '89
at their graduating exercises in
Music Hall,
Wednesday Morning, June 26th.

Mary Campbell Munson, Class of 1880

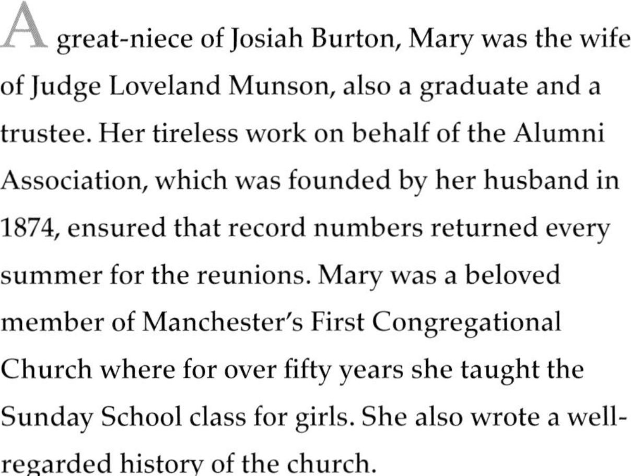

A great-niece of Josiah Burton, Mary was the wife of Judge Loveland Munson, also a graduate and a trustee. Her tireless work on behalf of the Alumni Association, which was founded by her husband in 1874, ensured that record numbers returned every summer for the reunions. Mary was a beloved member of Manchester's First Congregational Church where for over fifty years she taught the Sunday School class for girls. She also wrote a well-regarded history of the church.

Clara Hemenway, Class of 1892

A member of one of Manchester's leading families, Clara distinguished herself while a student at Burr and Burton, winning prizes in the Classical Department. Following graduation she became the first librarian at the new Mark Skinner Library in the Village. Funded by a gift from his daughter, the Mark Skinner Library opened in 1897. Clara also served as the first secretary of the Junior Alumni Association. She left Manchester for Hawaii in 1914 where she became librarian at the University of Hawaii.

Wilhelmina Hawley, Class of 1876

Anna Louise Simonds Orvis, Class of 1890

Wilhelmina Hawley and her cousin Julia were responsible for the establishment of the Manchester Historical Society in 1897. Their great-grandparents were early settlers in Manchester and their family at one time owned much of Equinox Mountain as well as a large farm south of Manchester Village. Wilhelmina became a college professor in Ohio, but she spent every summer at her home in Manchester Village.

Following graduation, Louise married Franklin Orvis's son George '88 and quickly became a leading light in Manchester society. She was the first woman to vote in Manchester and was for many years president of Manchester Village. Following her husband's death in 1917, Louise took over as president of the company that ran the Equinox House. Her husband had been a strong promoter of golf and was a founder of the Ekwanok Golf Club. Louise shared his interest, and in 1925 she established the Equinox Links Club, hiring Walter J. Travis to design the course.

Portrait of Reverend Joseph D. Wickham

Dr. Wickham's descendents still own his home in Manchester Village. The house, on the west side of Main Street, third down from the Equinox, was originally the Pierpont Tavern which was in operation during the 1790s.

Burr and Burton Seminary lost its most devoted supporter in 1891 when the Reverend Joseph D. Wickham died at age ninety-four. His success as a teacher was lovingly recounted by former students in numerous testimonials. But most important, perhaps, to the survival of the school was his success as a fundraiser. The trustees were reluctant to raise the tuition for fear it would make it impossible for students to attend. Though the tuition generally covered the yearly expenses of the school, there was never a surplus to cover necessary repairs and upgrades to the building. The solution was to periodically mortgage the property and Dr. Wickham would organize a subscription to pay it off.

His most interesting success came in 1882. By a strange twist of fate one of Wickham's classmates at Yale had been James Burr, a nephew of Burr and Burton's founder. Though James had died young, Wickham had remained friendly with his sisters and he must have made a good impression on them. In 1857, their father Isaac sold his farm in Manhattan, known as "The Pasture," for $1.1 million (the property was bounded by what is today Madison and Fifth between 41st and 44th Streets). In their wills, which had been drawn up in the early 1860s, Margaret and Mary Burr each left Burr and Burton $10,000, to be paid upon the death of the last surviving sister.

The Board of Trustees resisted the temptation to use part of the Burr legacies to fund the improvements so urgently needed in the 1880s. They decided instead to borrow $5,000 and repay the loan with interest from the permanent fund. In the summer of 1885, extensive improvements were made to the main building. The two most important, and the ones most likely to have an enormous impact on the everyday lives of the students, were the installation of a steam heating system and pipes for indoor plumbing. Interior blinds and shutters were hung in all the rooms and new furniture purchased as well. In 1888, further improvements were undertaken but electricity and the telephone would not be available for another twenty-five years.

For fifty years the tuition had changed very little. In the early years, students were charged $20 for tuition and $6 for room and board at a time when a five-pound bag of sugar cost ten cents. In 1883, tuition per year was $24 for the Classical and higher English curriculums, and room and board was $3.25 per week. Students were required to furnish their own linens, lamps, carpet, and toilet soap. By 1890, the trustees added an annual option: an all-inclusive package including tuition, room and board, books, and furnishings for a set fee of $300.

The times are no longer those of the early d… graduates will not question the wisdom of m… of the modern student, who prefers to develo… supplies of wood and water up two or three f…

Students and faculty, 1890

ys of the institution and probably the older king these provisions to meet the prejudice his muscle in other ways than by carrying ghts of stairs.

Loveland Munson at the 1890 Alumni Reunion

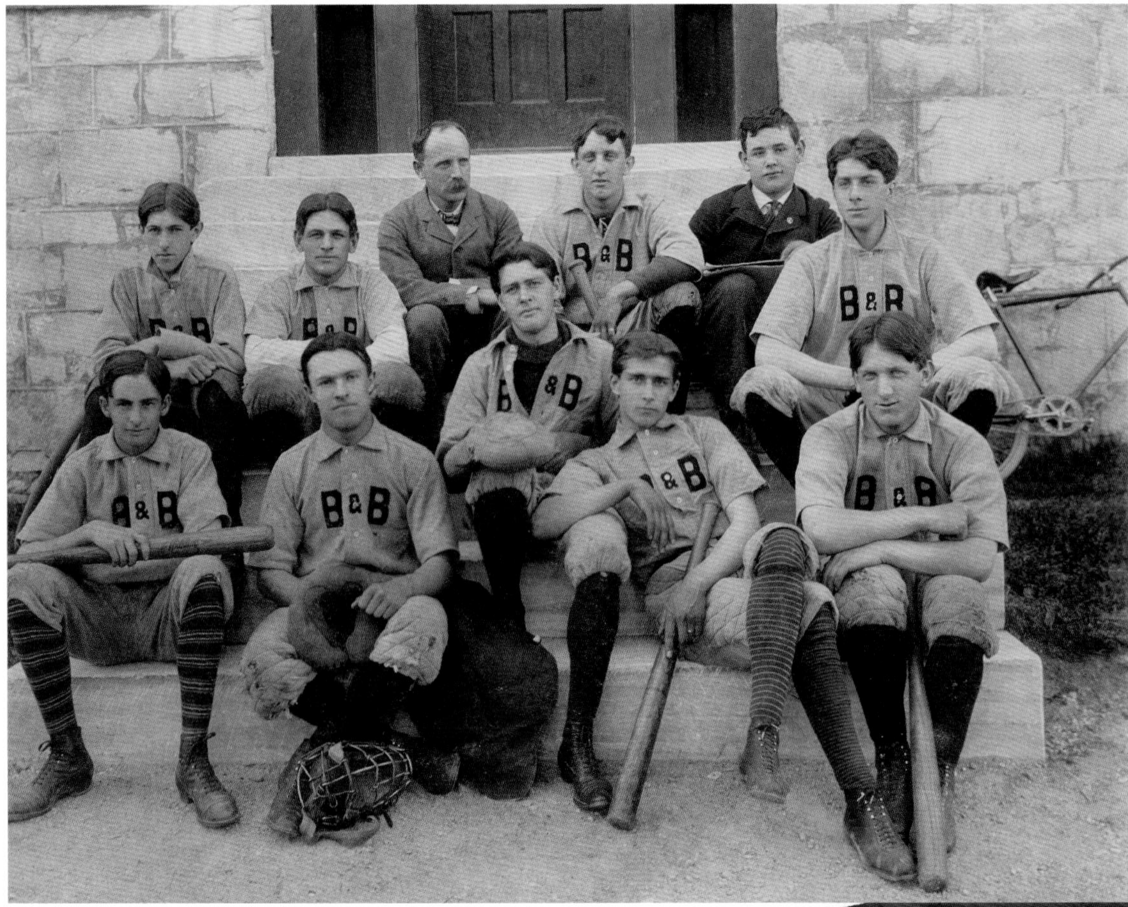

Baseball team, 1895

Twenty years after the first intercollegiate football game, organized sports teams began to appear in secondary schools. The first such sport to be mentioned in school literature is baseball in 1889. Initially listed with the other "societies," the Base Ball [sic] Association was composed of five officers, including the principal who was listed as "umpire." The association directed the activities of the Seminary Ball Club. Also mentioned are tennis and croquet.

The prohibition against playing baseball had disappeared from the school catalogs by the 1880s. It is tempting to conclude that this may have been influenced by the fact that two of the younger trustees, Loveland Munson and Dr. Lewis Hemenway, were key players on the Ondawa baseball team, Manchester's first baseball club.

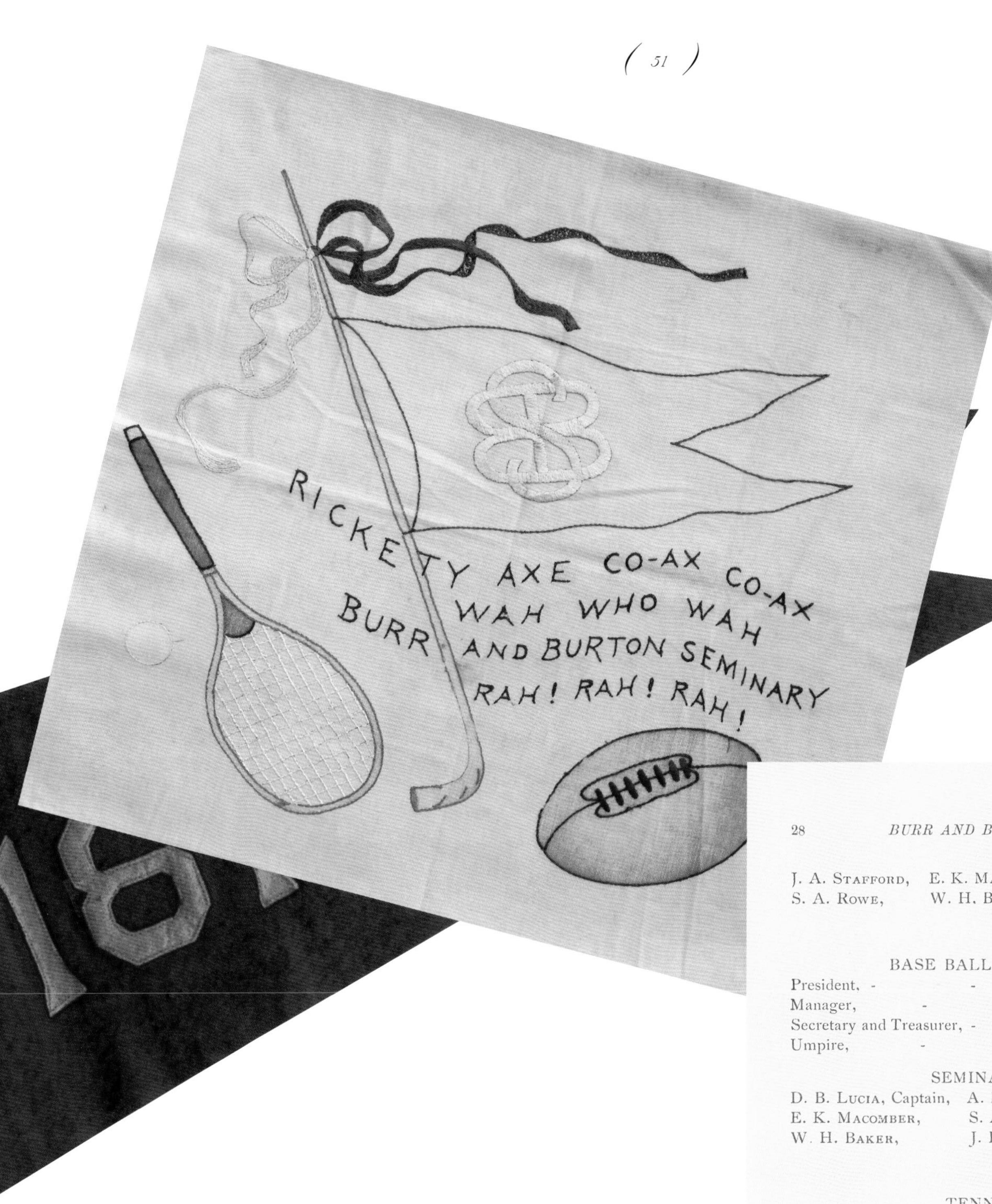

J. A. Stafford, E. K. Macomber, Edward McIntyre,
S. A. Rowe, W. H. Baker, Pianist.

BASE BALL ASSOCIATION.

President,	D. B. Lucia.
Manager,	The Principal.
Secretary and Treasurer,	Edward Griffith.
Umpire,	W. H. Everett.

SEMINARY NINE.

D. B. Lucia, Captain,	A. M. Lyon,	G. A. Martin,
E. K. Macomber,	S. A. Rowe,	J. Stafford,
W. H. Baker,	J. H. Minett,	E. R. White.

TENNIS CLUB.

President,	Prof. Moore.
Secretary and Treasurer,	W. H. Baker.

Rhetorical Contest, March 27th 1889.

DECLAMATION.

Gold Medal,	J. A. Stafford.
Silver Medal,	D. B. Lucia.

RECITATION.

Gold Medal,	Maude A. Sanford.
Silver Medal,	Jennie L. Goodenough.

The importance of physical exercise in school life is well recognized. Athletic sports are encouraged judiciously and the large grounds afford ample facilities for them; but it is the belief of the Principal that such sports should be well organized and under his direction. An excellent ball ground has been fitted up at considerable expense, which, with two tennis courts and a croquet ground, furnishes fine opportunities for out-of-door exercise.

Catalog, 1891

The North Chapel, 1890s

1894	Bell tower destroyed by cyclone
1894	Principal E. H. Botsford arrives from Williams College
1898	Junior Alumni Association formed
1899	New bell tower erected
1905	Football team wins first state championship
1913	New gymnasium dedicated
1929	Centennial celebrated with pageant

III *New Methods & Old Spirit*

1892 - 1929

The force of the wind sent the bell tower crashing onto the marble steps.

The cyclone did considerable damage to the principal's house and the wooden annex.

Seminary Building with original bell tower, 1892

In September 1894, a freak cyclone hit Manchester. A thoroughly unusual event in Vermont, the cyclone was brief but managed to do extensive damage to Burr and Burton and the north end of the Village. The original Gothic bell tower was ripped from the roof and crashed just in front of the main entrance. The roof of Seminary Building was also severely damaged as was the roof of the principal's house next door. The wooden annex, which had been added in 1862 to the south end of the main building, was also hit very hard. The trustees managed to find the money to repair the damaged roofs within a few months but the bell tower was an expensive proposition. The Junior Alumni Association undertook a subscription drive to raise the $500 necessary to replace the tower, but it was not until 1899 that the new tower and its bell were in place.

Students and faculty, 1894

Dr. Wickham was succeeded as president of the Board of Trustees by the Reverend Parsons Pratt, long-time pastor of the Dorset Congregational Church and a trustee since 1865. Five teachers were responsible for a curriculum that included natural science as well as the expected Greek, Latin, and English literature. The 1895 catalog describes the instruction given as "wide awake and progressive, so thorough and yet so cheap."

Mountain Day, 1895

The last decade of the nineteenth century was particularly energetic when it came to Manchester's cultural and educational institutions. Burr and Burton graduates led the way both in the community and at the school. Young alumni established the Junior Alumni Association which every year gathered alumni together for a reunion at the Equinox House. They were also the driving force behind the formation of the Manchester Historical Society and the Monday Club. When Mark Skinner's daughter decided to honor him by establishing a library for Manchester, it was Burr and Burton alumni who formed the organizing committee.

A graduate of Williams College, E. H. Botsford arrived as principal in the fall of 1894, bringing with him two teachers who would have a deep and abiding influence on Burr and Burton students and the community. Frances and Marcia Snyder had met Botsford during their years in Williamstown where they ran a school. During their six years at Burr and Burton, they developed lasting friendships with their students and inspired the kind of intense devotion only the very best teachers can. Active in the community as well, they were the founders of the Monday Club, a Manchester women's group interested in literature, still in existence today. In 1926, a group of alumni, spearheaded by members of the class of 1895, outfitted the living room in the original principal's house (at that time serving as a boys' dormitory) with comfortable furniture and artwork and dedicated the room to their memory. The plaque they installed is still affixed to the hearth.

Their teaching was not superficial. It was founded upon knowledge and animated by the spirit of investigation and acquisition of the very best thought of the world for present day enjoyment and practical use. There was no talk of cultural training, but they were the very soul of true culture, yet they were very human and understood the limitations of their pupils – pupil-friends. Unselfishness and devotion to their work were fundamental characteristics.

E. H. Botsford

Principal E. H. Botsford

Miss Fanny, as she was affectionately called by her students, was preceptress to the girls who boarded and taught mathematics, art, and drawing. Though she could be quite stern when required, Miss Fanny was well-known for her ability to find a way to inspire the most reluctant students. Her sister Marcia, who taught German, French, and English literature, was described by a former student as a "charming, delightful, sentimental, and wonderful teacher." Together they gave to the students of a small New England village all the benefits of their wide learning and cosmopolitan understanding of the world. When Botsford left in 1900 to take a position at Williams College, they retired to their home in Watertown, New York.

Frances and Marcia Snyder

Students and faculty, 1895

Class of 1895

There was in Manchester, that rich and fortunate village, an old co-educational day and boarding school of noble traditions; a private school for farmers' sons and daughters, democratic to the last degree, and with a tuition too tiny to be believed.

Sarah Cleghorn

"She was a poet, an educator – and a reformer." With these simple words, written in the introduction to her memoirs *Threescore*, the poet Robert Frost summed up the life work of his friend Sarah Cleghorn, the only Burr and Burton graduate to appear in Bartlett's *Quotations*. Though she was turned down for a teaching position at her alma mater after only one year at Radcliffe, Sarah never lost her love for the school. And though she taught for many years at the Manumit School, a progressive school in New York, she managed to remain exceptionally active with the Junior Alumni Association. Her spirited leadership contributed greatly to the successful fundraising campaign for the gymnasium built in 1913. And along with Mary Munson '80, she was the author of the pageant performed in 1929 to celebrate the 100th anniversary of the school's founding.

Sarah Cleghorn became quite well-known for her passionate devotion to socialism, pacifism, experimental education, and the abolition of capital punishment. She was that rarest of utopians – one who seriously lived by the principles she believed in and cherished her entire life.

Sarah Cleghorn

Sarah Cleghorn at graduation

Sarah Cleghorn, the author and teacher

While a student, Sarah excelled in English, Latin, and Greek, and impressed her fellow students not only with her sharp intellect but with her sweet and gentle disposition. Described as petite with a lovely complexion and blond hair, Sarah was nonetheless a fierce adversary of cruelty and stupidity. From her earliest years, her intense hatred of injustice set her apart. Though she never attained a college degree, Sarah published poems, essays, and novels. Her reputation brought her teaching assignments at Vassar and Wellseley as well as the friendship of distinguished writers of her time, including Frost and Dorothy Canfield Fisher. Sarah eventually became a Quaker and lectured for the Friends Council on Education. The most eloquent expression of her views on human misery and its remedies appears in her novel *The Seamless Robe*, published by Macmillan in 1945.

Loveland Munson, Class of 1862

Theodore Swift, Class of 1859

The Honorable Ahiman L. Miner

The son of Cyrus Munson, one of Burr Seminary's original founders, Judge Loveland Munson was elected to the Board of Trustees in 1873 when he was only twenty-nine years old. He served for forty-eight years, eleven years as president. Loveland studied law in the office of Elias B. Burton, also a president of Burr and Burton's Board of Trustees, eventually entering into partnership with him. In 1889, the Governor appointed him associate justice to the Supreme Court of Vermont, a position he ably filled for twenty-six years before being named Chief Justice in 1915. In 1874, he had been instrumental in founding the first Alumni Association. Principal James Brooks described him as the mainstay of the fundraising drive to build the gymnasium in 1912. Loveland Munson died in 1921 in the brick farmhouse on the rise between the Village and the Center in which he had been born.

A descendent of one of Manchester's first families, Theodore Swift was appointed to the Burr and Burton Board of Trustees in 1885 and served until his death in 1907. He was the proprietor for forty-one years of a landmark shop in the Village that stood beside the Equinox House. Originally known as Cone & Burton and later Cone & Swift, the store was moved across the street in 1908 and rebuilt as St. John's Chapel. Swift was a member of the Manchester Cornet Band in 1861, served in the state legislature in 1878, and was the first treasurer of the Manchester Historical Society formed in 1898.

Hon. Ahiman L. Miner, who was a trustee for over twenty-five years, was Manchester's most prominent citizen in the last quarter of the nineteenth century. Admitted to the bar in 1832, he held numerous political offices during his long life. Early in his career, he was among those who spoke at the Stratton Whig Convention with Daniel Webster in 1840. Though often considered a candidate for governor, he devoted his life to Manchester, a lawyer and judge who sat on the board of directors of every major institution in town.

Josiah Burton Hollister, Class of 1853

Named for his uncle, Josiah Burton Hollister was a vigorous and generous supporter of Burr and Burton. Elected to the Board of Trustees in 1873, he was named president in 1903. It was largely due to his efforts that the school attained fiscal stability at the turn of the century. In 1900, he offered $900 a year for three years to provide scholarships for needy students. He made a gift of $4,100 to the subscription drive to increase the endowment. It is estimated that he gave Burr and Burton $25,000 over his lifetime. When Loveland Munson announced at the 1903 Board of Trustees meeting that the subscription efforts had resulted in an endowment of $50,000, it is recorded that "Hollister and Severance rang the bell."

Edward Swift Isham

The Isham family was associated with Burr and Burton from its earliest years. The son of Bennington lawyer Pierpont Isham, Edward Swift Isham attended Burr Seminary in the late 1840s before leaving to graduate from Lawrenceville Academy and Williams College. As a young lawyer, he moved to Chicago where he formed a law partnership with Robert Todd Lincoln, Abraham Lincoln's only surviving son. Every summer Isham returned to Manchester to his home at Ormsby Hill. His son Edward Jr. was a trustee for many years and his grandson Lincoln Isham donated a science laboratory to the school in 1964.

Reverend Parsons Stuart Pratt

Reverend Parsons Pratt came to Vermont in 1856 to become the minister of Dorset's Congregational Church. In 1865 he was elected to Burr and Burton's Board of Trustees. Following the death of Dr. Wickham in 1891, he was elected president of the board and remained so until his resignation in 1903. As Dorset's pastor for forty years, Pratt was a well-respected member of the community. His interest in history led him to record the genealogies of all the families in his congregation. His diaries and meticulously kept church records form the basis for a rich and wide-ranging description of the Dorset community of his time.

INVITATION.

TO THE FORMER TEACHERS AND STUDENTS

OF

Burr and Burton Seminary.

In response to many earnest requests from those formerly connected with the Seminary, the Trustees, at their last annual meeting, voted to invite all the former Teachers and Students to

A RE-UNION

AT THE CLOSE OF THE PRESENT ACADEMIC YEAR.

THE ORDER OF EXERCISES WILL BE AS FOLLOWS:

A SOCIAL GATHERING, - At Music Hall, Tuesday Eve'g, June 27th.
At the Same Place, Wednesday, the 28th, at 10 o'clock, a. m.
AN ADDRESS OF WELCOME, - - - By Hon. A. L. Miner.
A HISTORY OF THE SEMINARY, - - By Rev. J. D. Wickham, D. D.
AN ADDRESS, - - By Rev. C. T. Woodruff, of Hudson, N. Y.
A POEM, By * * * * * * * *

In the Afternoon there will be a Dinner,

FOLLOWED BY

Speeches from Dr. Coleman, first Principal of the Seminary, and many others.

You are cordially invited to attend this Re-union.

We hope that a large number of the former Teachers and Students will be present, to renew the associations and revive the recollections of their pleasant school-days.

From those who cannot come, we shall be glad to receive letters.

Those to whom this circular is sent, are requested to extend the invitation to others formerly connected with the Seminary, or to forward to the Committee their address.

COMMITTEE OF ARRANGEMENTS.

J. D. WICKHAM, A. L. MINER, R. S. CUSHMAN, E. B. BURTON, L. A. AUSTIN.

Manchester, Vt., May 10, 1871.

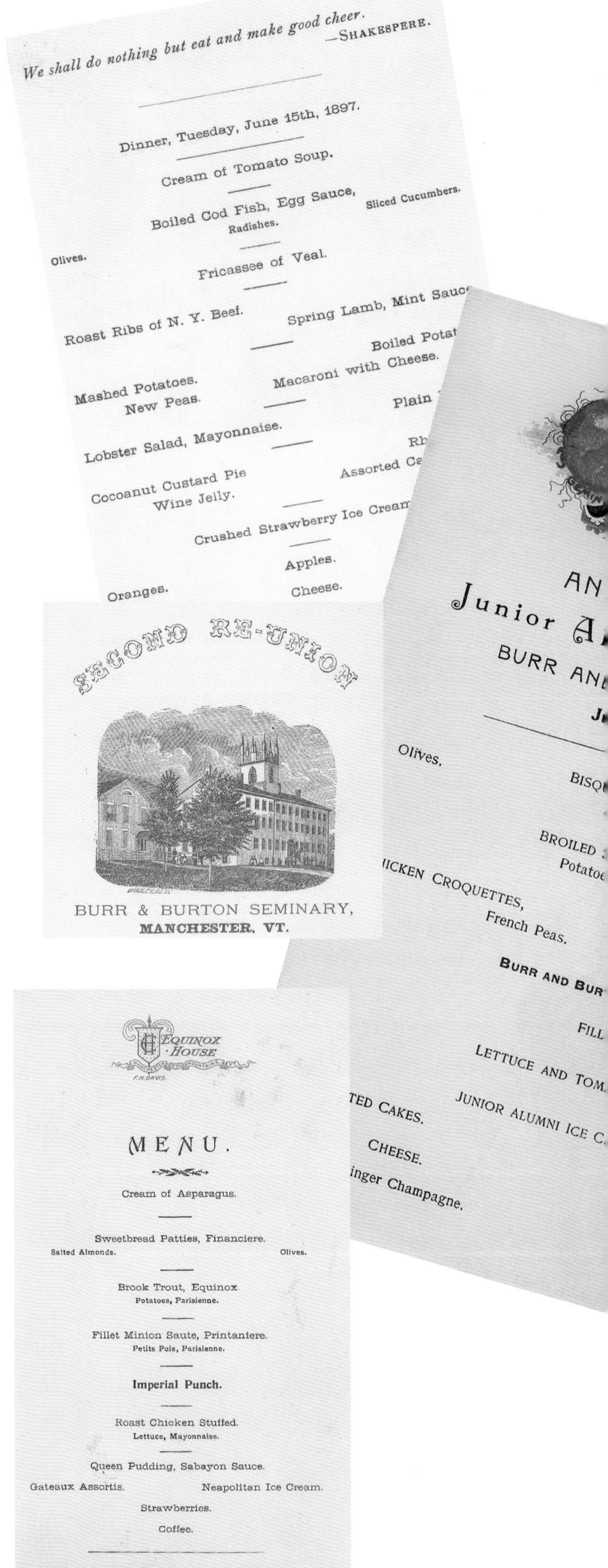

We shall do nothing but eat and make good cheer. —Shakespere.

Dinner, Tuesday, June 15th, 1897.

Cream of Tomato Soup.

Boiled Cod Fish, Egg Sauce,
Olives. Radishes. Sliced Cucumbers.

Fricassee of Veal.

Roast Ribs of N. Y. Beef. Spring Lamb, Mint Sauce

Mashed Potatoes. New Peas. Boiled Potat
Macaroni with Cheese.

Lobster Salad, Mayonnaise. Plain

Cocoanut Custard Pie. Wine Jelly. Assorted Ca

Crushed Strawberry Ice Cream

Oranges. Apples. Cheese.

SECOND RE-UNION

BURR & BURTON SEMINARY,
MANCHESTER, VT.

AN
Junior A
BURR AN

Olives.
BISQ
BROILED
Potato
ICKEN CROQUETTES,
French Peas.
BURR AND BUR
FILL
LETTUCE AND TOM.
JUNIOR ALUMNI ICE C.
TED CAKES.
CHEESE.
inger Champagne.

EQUINOX HOUSE

MENU.

Cream of Asparagus.

Sweetbread Patties, Financiere.
Salted Almonds. Olives.

Brook Trout, Equinox.
Potatoes, Parisienne.

Fillet Minion Saute, Printaniere.
Petits Pois, Parisienne.

Imperial Punch.

Roast Chicken Stuffed.
Lettuce, Mayonnaise.

Queen Pudding, Sabayon Sauce.
Gateaux Assortis. Neapolitan Ice Cream.
Strawberries.
Coffee.

BANQUET, JUNIOR ALUMNI ASSOCIATION
BURR AND BURTON SEMINARY,
JUNE 20TH, 1898.

By the time Burr and Burton had graduated its fortieth senior class, the trustees saw the wisdom of formally establishing an organization for former students that would sustain their interest in the school. Well-attended reunions had been held in 1866 and 1871. At the 1874 reunion it was decided to establish an Alumni Association, complete with a slate of officers. The next reunion, however, did not take place until 1883. By the 1890s, the trustees considered the alumni such a vital part of the school's success that for the first time they wrote a provision into the principal's contract requiring him "to increase the interest of the alumni in the welfare of the school."

The Equinox
Manchester
Vermont

...AL BANQUET
...nni Association,
...URTON SEMINARY,
...20th, 1899.

... LOBSTER.
...hes.
Salted Almonds.
...ON TROUT.
...enne.
...UNCH.
... BEEF WITH MUSHROOMS.
...S.
STRAWBERRIES.
COFFEE.

The Equinox
Manchester
Vermont

RE-UNION BANQUET
ALUMNI
OF
Burr and Burton Seminary
JUNE 27th, 1900, 2 P. M.
(67TH ANNIVERSARY)

CREAM OF CHICKEN B. AND B.
OLIVES
SALTED PEANUTS
FILLET OF HALIBUT, WICKHAM
HASHED POTATOES IN CREAM
CUCUMBERS
SWEETBREAD PATTIES, BULLARD
STRING BEANS
ALUMNI PUNCH
LAMB CHOPS, HOLLISTER
TOMATOES EN SURPRISE
ICE CREAM, "1900"
COFFEE
CAKES
EQUINOX GINGER CHA...

Burr and Burton Seminary.
REUNION, 1890.
ALUMNI DINNER AT EQUINOX HOUSE,
Thursday, June 26th, 1890.

Consommé, Royale.
Sliced Cucumbers.
Fillet of Bass, Tomato Sauce.
Potatoes Duchesse.
Boiled Turkey, Clam Sauce.
Roast Ribs of N. Y. Beef.
Roast Spring Lamb, Mint Sauce.
Chicken Croquettes with Peas.
Baked Macaroni with Cheese.
Shrimp Salad.
Mashed Potatoes.
New Beets.
Spinach.
Stewed Tomatoes.
Boiled Rice.
Raspberry Pie.
Custard Pie.
New England Indian Pudding.
Plain Rice Pudding, Hard Sauce.
Assorted Cake.
Danish Wine Jelly.
Assorted Nuts.
Raisins.
Buttermilk.
Crackers and Cheese.
Oranges.
Bananas.
Watermelons.
Coffee.
Crushed Strawberry Ice Cream.
Oolong Tea.

You are invited to attend the
Reunion of the Graduates and Old Students
of
Burr and Burton Seminary,
at Manchester, Vt., Thursday, June 26th,
1890.
Exercises in Music Hall at 9:30 A. M.
...nquet, at Equinox House, 3 o'clock P. M.

Ernest H. West '92 was master of ceremonies for many annual alumni dinners. In 1907, he took over the Norcrosse-West Marble Company in Dorset following his father's sudden death. The company was in the process of supplying marble for the construction of the New York Public Library in Manhattan. West sold the company in 1913 and went on to become Vermont's premier apple orchardist.

Reunions were held regularly during the 1890s. In 1898, a Junior Alumni Association was established for alumni from the class of 1890 and later classes. Older alumni were considered honorary members of the new association. The young alumni wanted to "instill new vigor into the main body of graduates and to aid Burr and Burton in whatever way we can." They began by raising the funds to replace the bell tower, making plans for future reunions, and embarking upon a fundraising project to raise money for a new gymnasium and athletic field. Alumnae Mary Campbell Munson, Anna Louise Simonds Orvis, and Sarah Cleghorn devoted themselves to finding alumni and making arrangements for the dinner which was always held at the Equinox House.

The girls' hall was accessible by a separate stairway and there was no communication with the main hall.

Teacher Lelia Bixby with boarding students, 1894

Though the boarding facilities remained essentially the same as fifty years earlier, the improvements made to the school in the 1880s meant that students in the 1890s were living more comfortably in their small dormitory rooms.

Students rose at 6:30 a.m. and began classes at 9 a.m. A midday break from noon to 1:15 preceded the afternoon sessions which ended at 3:30 p.m. Outdoor exercise occupied the time before supper at 6. From 7:30 until 9 students were in study hall. The retiring bell rang at 10 p.m.

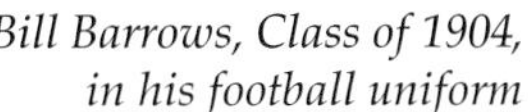

Bill Barrows, Class of 1904, in his football uniform

Bill Barrows and friends, 1904

By the mid-1890s, the student body was divided into four classes: the Senior Class, Junior Class, Sub-Junior, and First Year. There was also a Preparatory Class for those students who did not wish to attend the common school. With only seventy-two students in the entire school, classes were small, which was considered an advantage by the trustees. Over half of the seniors in 1896 went on to higher education with graduates attending such institutions as Yale, Amherst, Radcliffe, and the University of Vermont.

After Saturday classes ended, students were free to walk down to "the Street" to patronize the soda fountain at Hard's Drugstore. On Sunday they were all marched down to the First Congregational Church for services. Monday was still the weekly holiday.

The arrival of Mr. Botsford as principal in 1894 had a galvanizing affect on the athletic program at Burr and Burton. His keen interest in athletics is evidenced by the fact that he was the coach for both the football and the baseball teams.

Botsford also instituted the tradition of an annual field day, held at the Manchester Fairgrounds. Students competed in such events as the 880-yard-run, the two-mile bicycle race, the shot put, and the hammer throw.

Baseball was the school's first organized athletic team. A Base Ball [sic] Association was established to oversee the program with students as officers. In 1894, the first football team competed against Rutland and the Bennington YMCA, winning both games.

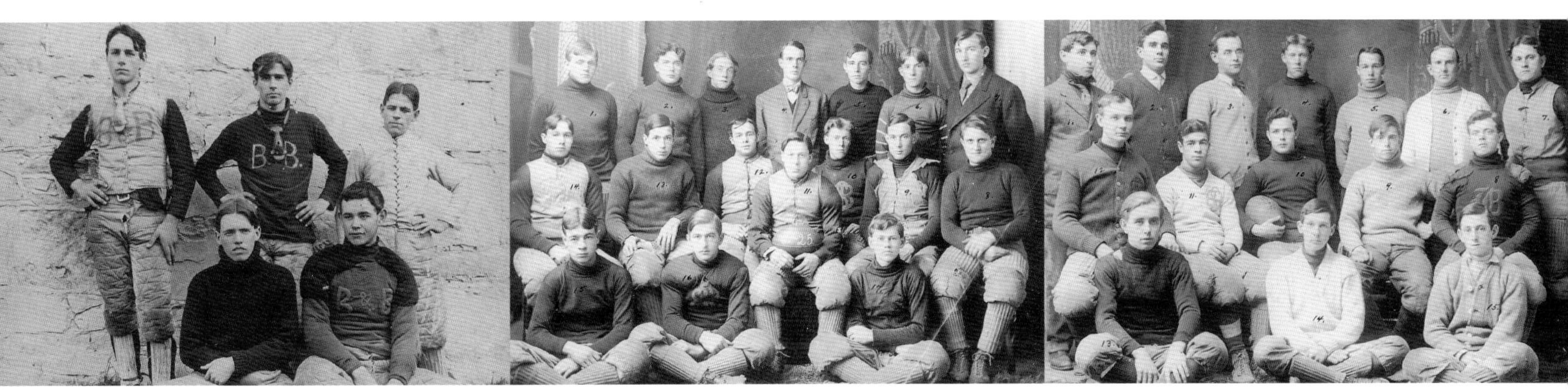

The 1905 and 1906 football teams were Vermont State Champions. The trustees voted in 1902 to "grade and fit up the pasture lands east of the Seminary for an athletic field," but it was only in 1925, with a gift of $25,000 from trustee and alumnus W. B. Pettibone, that the first field was built.

Class of 1900

It must be conceded that the people of this community have not been backward in meeting the past needs of the institution, and they can doubtless be relied upon to do their share in whatever may hereafter be undertaken for its advancement and prosperity. But it is evident that if the school is ever to be placed upon a financial basis like that enjoyed by some of the Seminaries in our State, the funds must come largely from friends of the institution who have greater means than are possessed by those permanently residing here.

Loveland Munson, president of the Board of Trustees, at the 1900 Alumni Reunion

Though Judge Munson was described as looking like a character out of Dickens, his old-fashioned frock coat and tall hat belied a keen interest in the future of Burr and Burton. Enrollment was still relatively low, but the school's financial health continued to improve in the first years of the twentieth century. The endowment would grow from $30,000 in 1895 to over $100,000 by 1912. Judge Munson attributed this to "the accession and liberality of many new friends of the Seminary as well as the continued devotion of those who may be styled its hereditary supporters. . . . The corporate designation of this institution perpetuates the names of its founders; but there are other donors of recent date who may well be accounted its preservers."

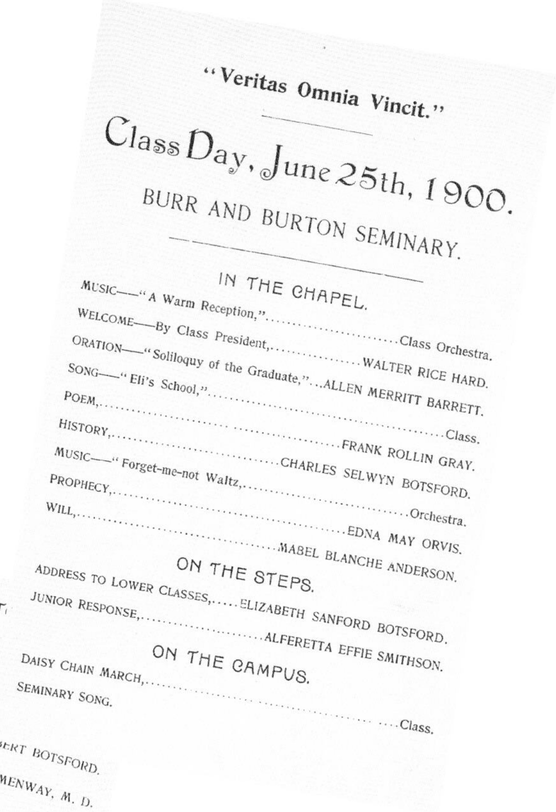

"Veritas Omnia Vincit."

Class Day, June 25th, 1900.

BURR AND BURTON SEMINARY.

IN THE CHAPEL.

MUSIC—"A Warm Reception,"........Class Orchestra.
WELCOME—By Class President,........WALTER RICE HARD.
ORATION—"Soliloquy of the Graduate,"...ALLEN MERRITT BARRETT.
SONG—"Eli's School,"........
POEM,........Class.
HISTORY,........FRANK ROLLIN GRAY.
MUSIC—"Forget-me-not Waltz,"........CHARLES SELWYN BOTSFORD.
PROPHECY,........Orchestra.
WILL,........EDNA MAY ORVIS.
........MABEL BLANCHE ANDERSON.

ON THE STEPS.

ADDRESS TO LOWER CLASSES,.....ELIZABETH SANFORD BOTSFORD.
JUNIOR RESPONSE,........ALFERETTA EFFIE SMITHSON.

ON THE CAMPUS.

DAISY CHAIN MARCH,........
SEMINARY SONG.
........Class.

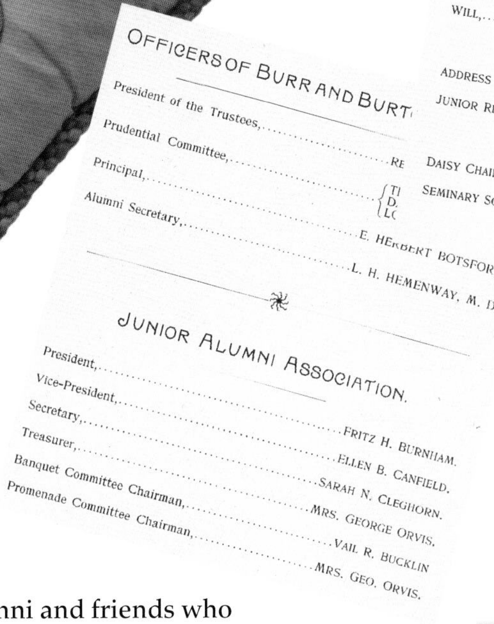

OFFICERS OF BURR AND BURT

President of the Trustees,........RE
Prudential Committee,........{T D. L
Principal,........E. HERBERT BOTSFORD.
Alumni Secretary,........L. H. HEMENWAY, M. D.

JUNIOR ALUMNI ASSOCIATION.

President,........FRITZ H. BURNHAM.
Vice-President,........ELLEN B. CANFIELD.
Secretary,........SARAH N. CLEGHORN.
Treasurer,........MRS. GEORGE ORVIS.
Banquet Committee Chairman,........VAIL R. BUCKLIN
Promenade Committee Chairman,........MRS. GEO. ORVIS.

These preservers were the alumni and friends who raised $50,000 for an endowment fund in 1903, including a $15,000 gift from Henry J. Willing of Chicago, son-in-law of the Honorable Mark Skinner. Preservation would remain a primary concern of the trustees. When Vermont mandated a secondary school education for all the state's children in 1905, Manchester, Dorset, and several surrounding mountain towns voted to tuition their students to Burr and Burton rather than add higher grades to the Manchester Center elementary school or build a new high school. The trustees welcomed this development as it would improve the school's financial stability, but they were also very aware of the unique advantages an independent school brought to the community. By 1909, students entering Burr and Burton were required to present a certificate of completion from their elementary school in order to qualify for the $24 in state aid to pay Burr and Burton's tuition.

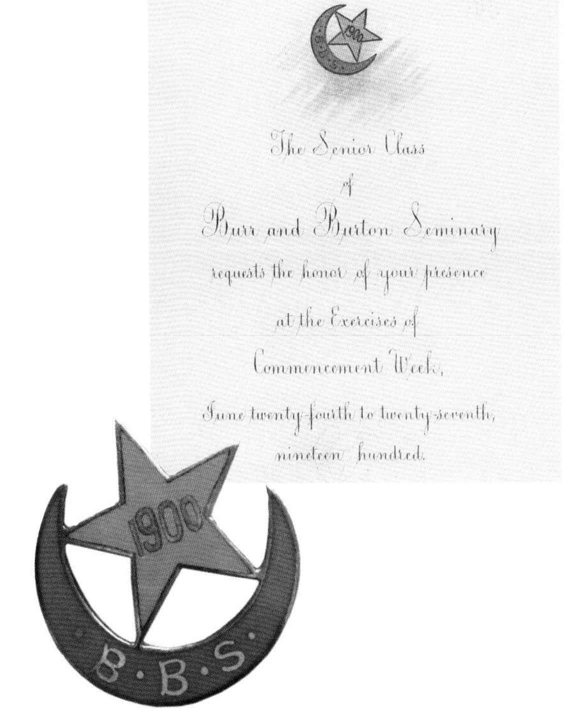

The Senior Class
of
Burr and Burton Seminary
requests the honor of your presence
at the Exercises of
Commencement Week,
June twenty-fourth to twenty-seventh,
nineteen hundred.

Mr. Hard had all the attributes of a hero. He was slow spoken, with a dry wit and a slight Vermont accent. He was gentle, but he could be decisive. He could make a small cooking fire with wet wood in deep snow, with one match. He could read trail marks and make his own snow shoes. He knew the woods and streams and meadows for thirty miles around. He was fascinated by people, especially oldtime Vermonters. Then and later, he made his poetry out of things and people at hand.

Robert R. R. Brooks, son of James Brooks,
Burr and Burton's principal, 1910-1919

Walter Rice Hard, a member of one of Manchester's oldest families, entered Burr and Burton in 1894 at the age of twelve. When he graduated in 1900, he was president of his class and bound for Williams College. Though he would one day be named poet laureate of Vermont and enjoy an international reputation, it was the breadth and depth of Hard's leadership that left a lasting impression on the school and the town. This had not been his original plan. When his father Jesse Hard suddenly died in 1902, Walter was forced to give up all hope for a college degree and return to Manchester to run the family drugstore. The strength of his character, liberally laced with high spirits and a self-deprecating sense of humor, quickly made him a popular and respected member of the community. Hard's Drugstore, located across from Equinox House, was the heart of village life. Many of the valley stories he turned into poems were first heard around the store's wood-burning stove and at the soda fountain. In addition to writing poetry, Hard found time to serve two terms as a state senator and run the Johnny Appleseed Bookstore. His abiding interest in his alma mater led him to become a leading force in the Alumni Association and later president of the Board of Trustees from 1941 to 1953. "Walter Hard is a great gentleman," said Headmaster E. H. Henry. "I have never met a finer or fairer person."

Walter Hard, Class of 1900

Walter Hard, circa 1920

Hard's Drugstore, 1930s

Walter Hard

Margaret Steele Hard

Literary critic Louis Untermeyer ranked Walter Hard among the top thirty poets since 1776. Carl Sandburg wrote that he and Walter were "of the same school in believing that an anecdote of sufficient pith and portent is in essence a true poem." Walter Hard published eight volumes of poetry and contributed poems to numerous periodicals. Together with his wife he wrote *This Is Vermont*, a fond description of life in his beloved home state.

Margaret Steele was a beautiful young woman from Philadelphia whose family summered in Manchester. She and Walter first met at a party given by her mother for local residents, and in 1912 they married. Their two children, Walter Hard, Jr. and Ruth Hard Bonner, would also graduate from Burr and Burton. Ruth '28 was the founder of the Johnny Appleseed Bookstore which Walter and Margaret took over in 1935 after selling the drugstore. Her brother Walter '33 was for many years the editor of *Vermont Life* magazine.

Chick Evans (front right) and the Burr and Burton baseball team, 1906

Chick Evans was the first and only Burr and Burton graduate to play for a major league baseball team. Charles Franklin Evans, born in 1889 in Arlington, Vermont, graduated from Burr and Burton in 1907. While a student, he was well-known as the star pitcher and captain of the baseball team. "The battery work this year is such as never before been exhibited on these grounds," wrote the athletic editor of the 1906 *Burtonian*. "Captain Evans has been a power in the box that all opposing teams found was not to be trifled with . . . Evans has done great batting this year."

Chick Evans (front right) and the Burr and Burton baseball team, 1905

During his years at Burr and Burton, Evans matched up several times with legendary pitcher Ray Fisher who played for Middlebury High School. In 1908 they became teammates when Evans was picked up by the Hartford national league team after being spotted at a semipro game in Hoosick Falls. During the 1908 season he won thirteen games for Hartford, but they sold him in 1909 to the Boston Doves. Opening day of the 1910 season Evans pitched a one-hit ball over the last three innings to pick up the 3-2 win against the New York Giants but then his baseball career stalled. His last outing against major league competition took place in Vermont at a Columbus Day baseball contest between rival towns Bennington and Hoosick Falls. Evans had been hired by Hoosick Falls, but Bennington had hired the Boston Red Sox. The game was an 11-1 rout. His career went downhill soon after as did his health. Evans died in 1916 at age twenty-six and is buried in Bennington.

Class of 1910

The object of this Institution, so rich in traditions of past usefulness, is to combine all that is best in the modern high school, including its organization, discipline, and practical efficiency, with the noble educational ideal of the traditional New England Academy with its emphasis on culture and character.

Catalog, 1909

In the early years of the twentieth century the curriculum gradually changed to reflect the needs of the times. In addition to the college preparatory classes and academic subjects, students could now choose a business course "covering all the ground usually covered in Business College," which included stenography, typewriting, bookkeeping, as well as commercial arithmetic, law, and geography.

Board was still $3.50 a week and room rent $5 a term. A Remington typewriter could be rented for $2 a term. Electric power was installed in 1907 and students were charged extra for its use.

Bill Wilson (left) with classmates

William G. Wilson is probably the best-known person of the thousands who have attended Burr and Burton over the years. He never graduated, but while there he developed a determined spirit that grew stronger and stronger and eventually won him fame and the praise of millions of people around the world.

His grandfather enrolled him in Burr and Burton as a boarding student early in the spring of 1909. On the baseball diamond one day, a boy threw a ball that hit and knocked Bill down. When he got up all the boys were laughing at him. His determination awoke and he shouted back at them, "I'll show you." And show them he did, first teaching himself to throw a curve and then a spitball. The next year he was the team's pitcher, and the year after was also captain of the team. Baseball wasn't his only sport. He went out for football and was the team's best punter. Being shy and believing he was homely and clumsy, Bill showed no interest in girls until his junior year. Then he became very interested in Bertha Bamford, the daughter of the Rev. W. H. Bamford, the Episcopal minister in Manchester. Soon he fell in love with her. All that spring and summer they were very close, seeing each other nearly every day.

In November 1912, Bertha went on a three-day trip to New York with her parents. Because she had promised to write to him, he stopped at the post office in the morning two days after she left, hoping without success for a letter from her. He hurried on to Burr and Burton but was late. The students were already singing at morning chapel. At the close of the hymn, Mr. Brooks, the principal, rose, reached in his pocket, and took out a piece of yellow paper, a telegram. Then he told the students news that would leave Bill depressed for the next three years. Mr. Brooks had received a telegram from New York City saying Bertha had died the night before, November 18, 1912, following an operation in Fifth Avenue Hospital.

Bill was devastated. He failed nearly all of his midyear exams, so that by spring it was obvious that, despite being president of the senior class, he would not graduate. And Bertha still lived in his brain. So he left school and went to Boston to live with his mother.

Roger Griffith, Class of 1937

Bill Wilson (right) and Bertha Bamford with friend

Bill Wilson and Bertha Bamford (left)

As co-founder of Alcoholics Anonymous, Bill Wilson would have a profound influence on the lives of millions of people. But this would not have been predicted during his years as a student at Burr and Burton where he was a popular student and admired athlete. Wilson should have graduated with the Class of 1913, but the unexpected death of a classmate and dear friend left him unable to concentrate and he did not finish his senior year.

The writer Aldous Huxley considered Bill Wilson to be "the greatest social architect of the twentieth century." *Time* magazine named him one of the ten most influential people of the twentieth century.

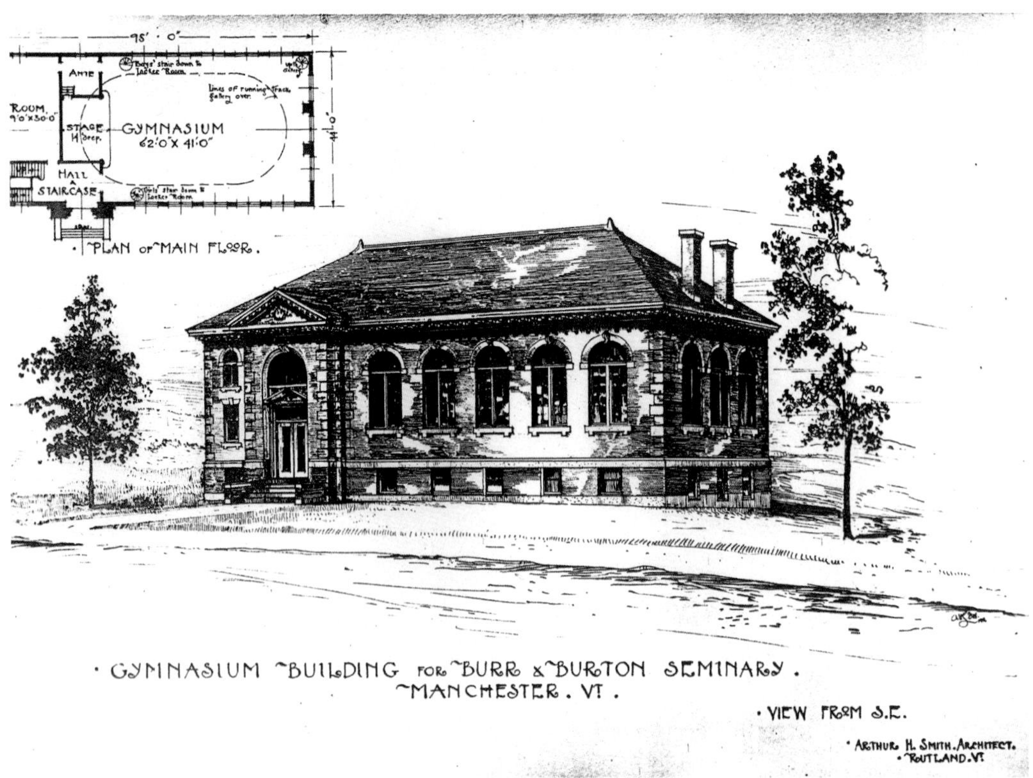

Architect's drawing of the new gymnasium, 1912

The need for an additional building that could serve as a gymnasium and an assembly hall had been recognized by the Class of 1890. They decided to form an association to raise the necessary funds. Subsequently, the Junior Alumni Association took over the task of raising money to achieve this goal. But it was not until 1911 that the trustees embarked upon the school's first fundraising campaign to raise the $15,000 necessary to finance construction. After receiving a $5,000 challenge grant from a "lady" who was not identified, the trustees made an appeal to "public-spirited persons, both residents and non-residents" to "help in proportion to their ability." In their statement setting out the case for the new building, the trustees emphasized their belief that this new facility was essential to the school's future success. Many of the gifts received were from alumni, including Sarah Cleghorn '95, Walter Hard '00, George W. Burton '73, and the Pettibone brothers. Generous gifts also came from community members, including a handsome donation from Robert Todd Lincoln, who spent every summer at Hildene, the home he had built in Manchester Village just seven years earlier.

First basketball team, 1914

On July 7, 1913, Principal James Brooks led the dedication ceremonies for the new gymnasium. A. Phelps Wyman, an alumnus of the school and a landscape architect in Chicago, provided the original plans which were carried out by A. H. Smith, a local architect. The general contractor was Hiram Eggleston of Manchester, who charged the trustees far less than any of the other contractors bidding on the job. He received much public appreciation for his generosity and his good workmanship. "From basement wall to chimney cap-stone, it has been built on honor," Brooks told the assembled guests. "No important detail has been slighted. No shoddy material used. . . . I take off my hat to honest work and an honest man. All unwitting our citizen contractor has built for himself a lasting monument to his memory."

Roger Conant Perkins, Class of 1913

Following his graduation from Burr and Burton, Roger Perkins left Manchester to attend Amherst College from which he graduated in 1917. On April 9, 1917, three days after war had been declared against Germany, Roger joined the Naval Reserve Force. After completing coursework at the Massachusetts Institute of Technology, he was assigned to flight school in Key West, Florida. On March 13, 1918, he was killed during a test run when his plane inexplicably fell to the ground and crashed.

Clifford Copping , Class of 1910

Clifford Copping has given his life in the cause of freedom. He died courageously, a true soldier. How well we all remember his great popularity among us, his unbounded good spirits, his cheerful disposition. He was a great favorite with all who knew him and recognized by all as an unusually fine fellow. No one ever knew him to do a mean or unmanly thing, on the field of sports or off. "Cop," as he was familiarly called, knew not the meaning of the word "defeat," and there we may find the secret of his successful life.

Louis W. Batchelder, Class of 1910

The Class of 1928 included several second- and third-generation graduates such as Mildred Orton, Ruth Hard, and James Campbell

Madison Bates, our principal, loved Mountain Day. He would have the biggest smile on his face. The entire school would spend the day hiking somewhere – Dorset quarry, or Prospect Rock or Table Rock on Mount Equinox. This was the only time we girls could wear pants. We all wore hiking pants. We enjoyed it, but Mr. Bates most of all.

Mildred Wilcox Orton, Class of 1928

Following their marriage, Mildred Wilcox and her husband Vrest Orton moved to Weston, Vermont, in 1936. After wartime service in Philadelphia and Washington, D. C., the couple moved back to Weston in 1946 where they founded the Vermont Country Store and raised their two sons. Lyman graduated from Burr and Burton in 1959, and Jeremy graduated in 1962. The Vermont Country Store is still flourishing under the direction of the next generation of Ortons.

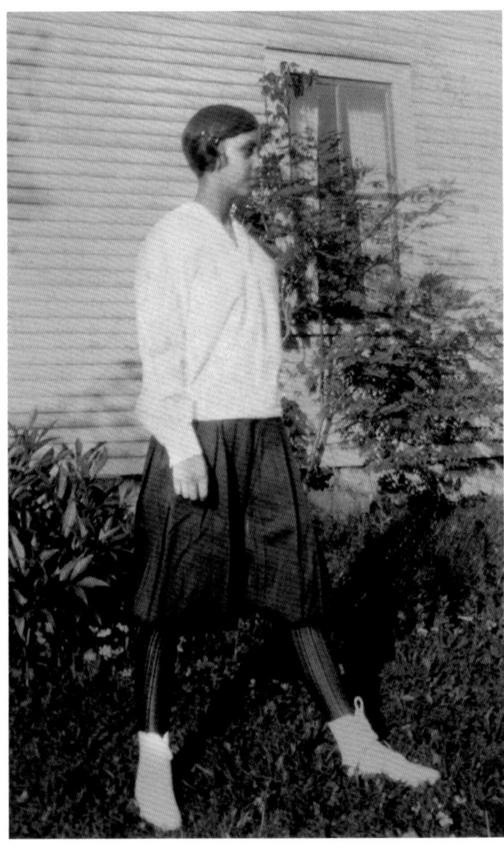

Mildred Wilcox, Class of 1928, in the required gym uniform

Observatory and Lincoln telescope, 1928

Mary Harlan Lincoln, 1868

In April 1928, following the death of her husband Robert Todd Lincoln, Mary Harlan Lincoln presented his telescope to Burr and Burton Seminary along with the funds to construct and maintain a duplicate of the Hildene observatory on the hillside overlooking the school's playing fields.

Not long after he completed his beloved Hildene in 1904, Lincoln built a small brick observatory to the east of the main house overlooking the valley. In 1909, Mr. Lincoln installed in his observatory an eight-foot equitorial telescope that had been custom-made for him by the well-known firm of Warner and Swasey of Cleveland, Ohio. The telescope cost Mr. Lincoln $1,900 and took six months to make. It was at the time the finest telescope available in the world.

Mary Harlan Lincoln was married to Robert Todd Lincoln, the only child of President Abraham Lincoln and Mary Todd Lincoln to survive to adulthood, in 1868. Though they made their home in Chicago, the family spent every summer at Hildene.

When the Friends of Hildene completed their task of bringing Mr. Lincoln's house to life again in 1976, it seemed only fitting to Burr and Burton's trustees that the telescope belonged in its original home and so it was officially returned in 1992.

1829

Burr and Burton celebrated the 100th anniversary of its founding with a pageant that was straight out of Wilder's play "Our Town." Written by Sarah Cleghorn '95 and Mary Campbell Munson '80, the pageant was composed of fifteen "episodes" chronicling the story of Burr and Burton from its founding to the present. The actors portraying the historical characters were not only students but trustees, teachers, and many members of the community. Walter Hard was Mr. Burr, trustee George W. Burton played his ancestor Josiah Burton, and Judge Griffith acted as Mr. William Burnham. Woven throughout were the songs appropriate to each time frame represented in the episode. The musical component of the entire program was under the direction of Mrs. Carl Ruggles, whose husband would soon become as lauded an American composer as his friend Charles Ives.

The pageant almost did not take place. "Except for the ingenuity of Messrs. Edward J. and Henry Markey and Otis Brooks, the whole event would have been a failure because of the lack of electric lights. A severe thunder storm late in the afternoon of the day of the production had crippled the power service. These men pressed into service a farm lighting outfit and provided lights for the stage, so that the pageant was produced with but a short delay."

Burtonian, 1930

Students and faculty, 1929

1929 1929

Photograph by Clara Sipprell, 1940s

1934	Seniors wear blue caps and gowns at commencement exercises
1943	E. H. Henry named headmaster
1947	Football team wins state championship
1958	Boys' varsity basketball team wins first state championship
1965	New classroom wing completed

IV *Sound Character & Purpose*

1930 – 1969

This year is evidently going to be a bad one for the school financially. The cost of the repairs to the heating plant is much more than expected and if we lose $3,500 in tuitions in addition, it will be a sad story at the next annual meeting of trustees. Guess I better stay away!

George W. Burton '73, president of the Board of Trustees, letter to the school's business manager Paul Bullock, 1935

In the first decade of its second century, Burr and Burton continued to struggle with low enrollments and inadequate financial resources. But the school also continued to be fortunate in its headmasters: Both F. Beacom Rich and Ralph Howes were highly educated men who also found time to coach athletic teams. Also fortunate was the small student body that required only twelve teachers. Although the school year continued to revolve around the classroom, athletic contests, seasonal dances and parties, and traditional celebrations such as Class Day, the worldwide economic depression had its impact: From 1933 to 1937 the annual alumni banquet was canceled "because of the expense it entails."

The decade saw many firsts. The 1934 graduates wore blue caps and gowns at commencement for the first time. In 1936, the first field hockey team was organized. Green and gold school colors appeared in the 1937 *Burtonian* for the first time, and the following year the term "Bull Dogs" made its debut in the sports section. In 1939 the first ski team took to the slopes and senior photographs appeared in the *Burtonian*, which for the first time looked more like modern yearbook than a literary magazine.

As graduates of Burr and hope that we shall be in an promote its welfare.

Class of 1939

f Burton Seminary . . . we
even better position to help

Don Powers, 1937 Class President, Class Day Speech

Paul Bullock became assistant headmaster in the 1936 and acted as business manager for the school until his retirement in 1969.

In winter, students and faculty members gathered at noon near the marble steps. Mr. Bullock would show up carrying his jack-jump with its one runner and small wooden seat, making it something to be ridden only by those with the best of balance or the worst of intelligence. With cries of encouragement from his audience he would hop aboard and start down the fast snow-packed path going faster and faster. With any luck there would be no cars coming up or down the road and he would shoot across safely and be home for lunch in a matter of seconds. The watching noon crowd never grew smaller. What they really wanted was to see Mr. Bullock, just once at least, fall. He never did.

Roger M. Griffith '37

The austere Paul Bullock, who would spend forty-eight years of his life as a teacher at Burr and Burton, was the energetic head of the Commercial Department, which had been introduced in 1921 to provide non-college-bound students with all the skills necessary to enter the business world. Every spring he would tap the maples on the school's sloping front lawn and teach the students how to make maple syrup.

From the earliest years, the school's weekly break began at noon on Saturday and included Sunday and Monday. By the 1930s, the holiday had become Saturday and Sunday with the half-day preserved on Friday, a tradition that continues seventy-five years later.

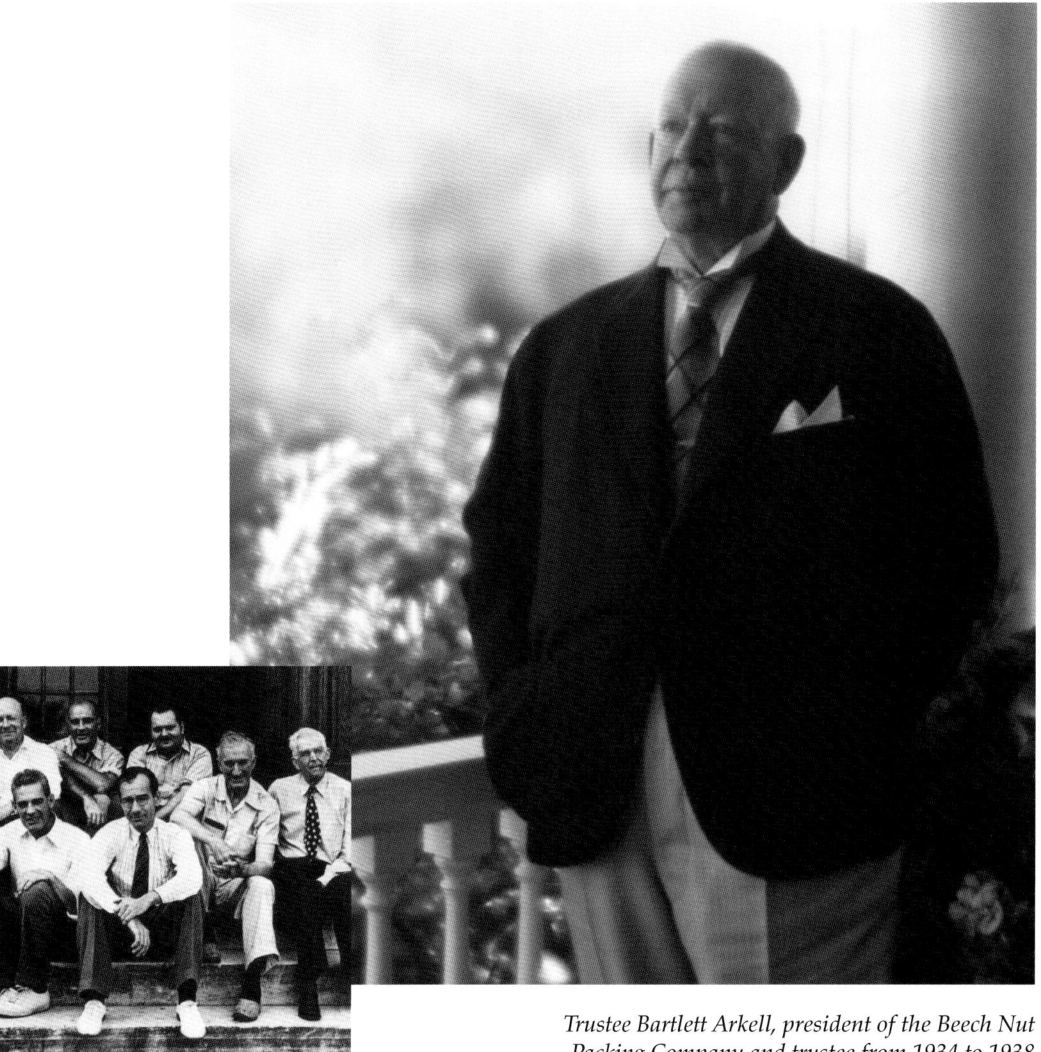

Trustee Bartlett Arkell, president of the Beech Nut Packing Company and trustee from 1934 to 1938

Some of the original members of Southern Vermont Artists, Inc., on the steps of the gymnasium in the 1930s

Of the eleven men and one woman who formed Southern Vermont Artists, Inc., in 1934, four were graduates of Burr and Burton and two were trustees. Anna Louise Simonds Orvis '90, Walter Hard '00, Ernest West '92, Judge Edward Griffith '88, and Bartlett Arkell were instrumental in founding the artists' organization that would oversee the development of the Southern Vermont Arts Center. Walter Hard, then president of the Alumni Association, was especially helpful in promoting and organizing the artists' exhibitions. The Southern Vermont Artists Annual Exhibitions were held in the school's gymnasium (now the Riley Center for the Arts) from 1934 until 1950. These exhibits were a great boon to Manchester's reputation, drawing national recognition. Hard is also credited with the suggestion that a group of supporters be organized to underwrite the cost of the art shows. The Friends of the Southern Vermont Artists provided not only financial support but organizational continuity as well. Arkell was one of the most generous supporters of this group. Though only a summer resident of Manchester Village, Bartlett Arkell had a lasting influence on the community. In addition to supporting the Southern Vermont Artists and the students of Burr and Burton, Arkell donated to the town the land that is today the recreation park.

Joseph Fowler, Class of 1935

Joseph Fowler '35, the fourth generation of the Fowler family to attend Burr and Burton, was among the dozens of Burr and Burton graduates who joined the armed forces during the Second World War. He left Vermont for Texas in 1943 where he received his basic training in the U. S. Army. He initially was assigned to two field artillery units, which later took considerable casualties in Europe. But he had been transferred to the 1155th Howitzers and sent to Hawaii. His battalion would have been among the first wave to land had the United States decided to invade the Japanese mainland. Fortunately for Joe and his family, the war ended before this was necessary. Joe's older brother Harvey '34, serving with the Marine Corps, was killed on Guam in 1944. The Manchester VFW post is named in his honor.

Lawrence Burton Wilcox, Class of 1938

Lawrence Wilcox '38 was the Manchester Selective Service Board's candidate for enlistment in the U. S. Army in 1942. Not long after joining up, he was tapped for Officer's Candidate School and then assigned to the 1880th Engineer Aviation Battalion as Battalion Motor Officer. In 1943, the 1880th made the long trip by sea to India where they spent the war years constructing the strategic overland supply route from India to China known as the Ledo and Burma Road, a project considered to be one of the engineering marvels of the modern world. Not even the worst mud season in Vermont could have prepared him for the rain and mud they encountered, but they completed the road in only two years. First Lieutenant Lawrence Wilcox returned to Vermont in 1946.

Headmaster E. H. "Al" Henry (with Maggie) said, "We were a happy school, a tight school, well-disciplined. My philosophy was to keep 'em busy."

The 1947 football team won the state championship in their division.

I remember him as being brilliant. He was direct and could be stern, but he was also very understanding and gentle.

Barbara Bardin, Class of 1969

When the trustees were faced with finding a new principal in 1943, they were very clear about the qualifications: "He must be an organizer, an administrator, and a counselor. His wife must be adequate for the position." They could not have found a more perfect candidate than E. H. Henry. Al Henry came to Burr and Burton as the twenty-second headmaster in 1943. A 1939 graduate of Middlebury College, he broke his neck in a football scrimmage his freshman year. Though this spelled the end of his career as a player, he managed to fulfill his keen interest in football by coaching. One of his first acts as headmaster was to reestablish football as a varsity sport after a twenty-eight-year hiatus. The first year the team lost all its games, but in the third year Burr and Burton won the Division I state championship.

When Al Henry arrived, enrollment was only 120 students, a quarter of whom were weekly boarders. By the time he retired in 1969, enrollment had reached 396, the dormitory had been transformed into a modern chemistry lab, and two buildings had been added to the campus, thanks to the philanthropy of his friend Sarah Given Larson. He also established drama and music activities with the help of his wife Ruth. Mr. and Mrs. Henry were deeply dedicated to Burr and Burton and were well-respected members of the Manchester community.

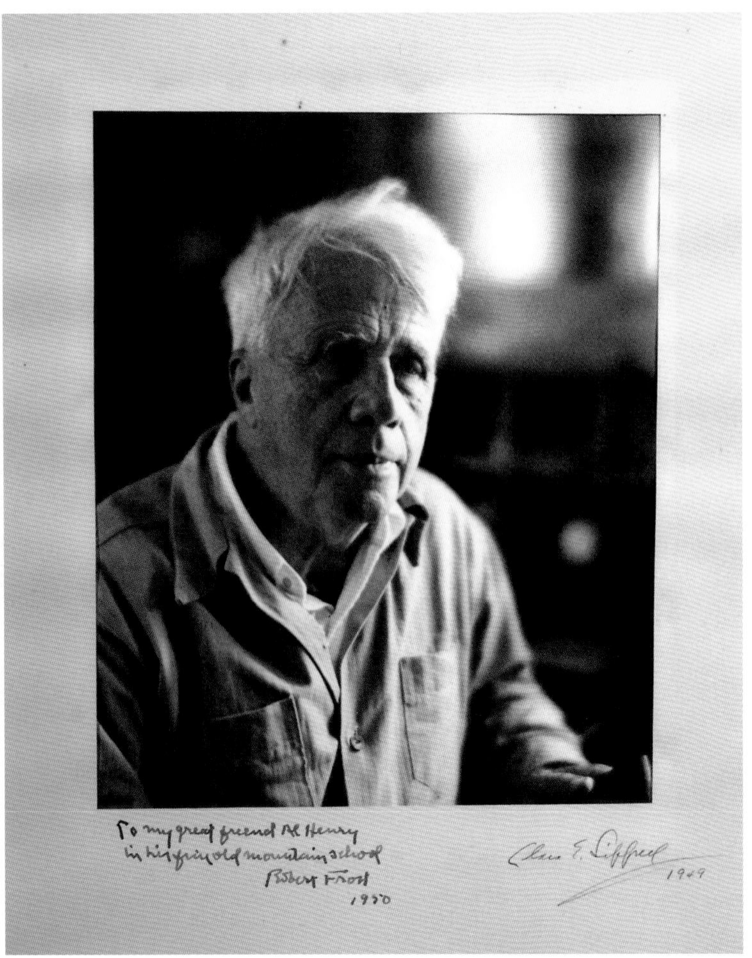

Robert Frost photographed by Clara E. Sipprell in the 1940s. This photograph appeared as the frontispiece in The Complete Poems of Robert Frost 1949.

Al Henry met Robert Frost at Middlebury College's Bread Loaf Writers' Conference that Frost attended every summer. In the early 1940s, Al Henry was in charge of operations at Bread Loaf. The two became good friends and although Frost was only a summer visitor to Vermont during these years, he accepted his friend's invitation to address the graduating class in 1947 and again in 1949.

Two Vermont poets: Walter R. Hard and Robert Frost, 1962

Al Henry inspired friendship with numerous contemporaries, including poets Walter Hard and Robert Frost. These two poets who wrote about what Frost called "country matters" had surprisingly never met before they were brought together by Al Henry for the first time in 1962. Walter Hard wrote, "Robert Frost has the genius of a poet. Al Henry has the genius of friendship." Son Peter Henry '60 believes his father's many friendships were the result of his being "serious-minded, with no pretensions, and in possession of an easy sense of humor."

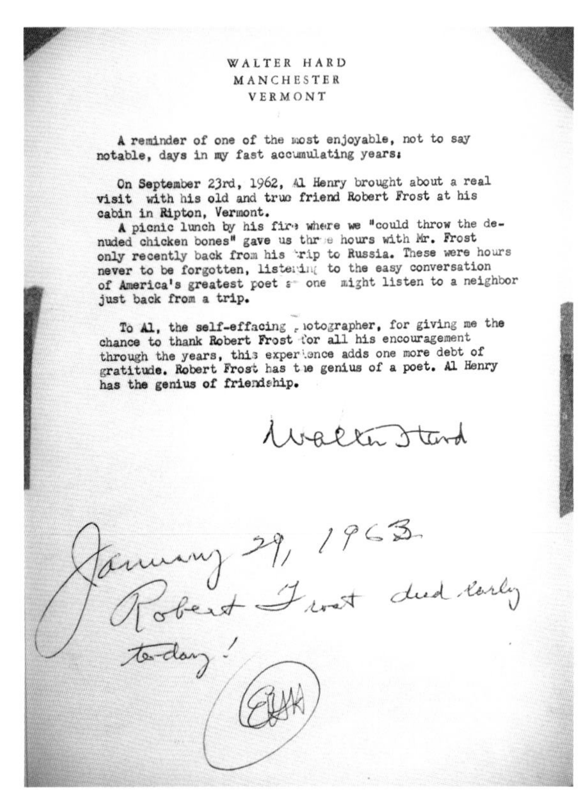

WALTER HARD
MANCHESTER
VERMONT

A reminder of one of the most enjoyable, not to say notable, days in my fast accumulating years:

On September 23rd, 1962, Al Henry brought about a real visit with his old and true friend Robert Frost at his cabin in Ripton, Vermont.

A picnic lunch by his fire where we "could throw the denuded chicken bones" gave us three hours with Mr. Frost only recently back from his trip to Russia. These were hours never to be forgotten, listening to the easy conversation of America's greatest poet as one might listen to a neighbor just back from a trip.

To Al, the self-effacing photographer, for giving me the chance to thank Robert Frost for all his encouragement through the years, this experience adds one more debt of gratitude. Robert Frost has the genius of a poet. Al Henry has the genius of friendship.

Walter Hard

January 29, 1963.
Robert Frost died early to-day!

In this letter to Mr. Henry, Hard expresses his appreciation for bringing about the meeting with Frost.

Mr. Henry established a tradition of giving honor roll students a holiday on both the first day of deer-hunting season in November and the opening day of the fishing season in May. Unfortunately for future students, this was one tradition that did not impress future headmasters.

Anna Louise Simonds Orvis '90 is credited as one of the first to see the economic potential that winter sports offered to Manchester. As the proprietor of Equinox House, Mrs. Orvis followed in her father-law's footsteps as a promoter of institutions and events that would bring tourists to Manchester. Organized winter sports first appeared in Manchester in the 1930s with the formation of the Winter Sports Club. Community members cut ski trails, built a skating rink and bobsled runs, and hosted a winter carnival and dog sled races. But it wasn't until the ski areas Snow Valley and Big Bromley were completed in the 1940s that snow became white gold for southern Vermont communities. Burr and Burton students were quick to take up the new sport. Ski teams were organized for both boys and girls. Mike McCooey '53 remembers being released from school early so that he and his friends could use snowshoes to pack the ski runs. By the 1950s, Burr and Burton skiers were dependable members of Bromley's ski patrol.

Downtown Manchester during ski season, circa 1950

MY INN
RMONT
Lifts
NS IN THE E

Burr and Burton ski team, 1947

Early advertisements for the first ski resorts in Southern Vermont

English teacher John Fay

By the time John Fay arrived as the College Preparatory English teacher, Burr and Burton no longer offered Greek to its college-bound students, but the school's dedication to a serious college preparatory education remained strong. Exacting teachers like Fay and Alison Boright gave their students a thorough grounding in the essential elements of English grammar, composition, and literature, and inspired an enduring devotion in their students.

Burr and Burton's first championship basketball team

They did not gain this title by chance. They won it by sheer force of fine playing and a determination to win.

G. S. Bennett '11, editor of the *Manchester Journal*

Before the age of televised sports, high school athletic contests drew huge crowds and Manchester was no exception. The school band paraded up Seminary Avenue before football games and Friday night basketball games provided much-appreciated community entertainment during the long winter. In March 1958, 500 Manchester residents traveled to Middlebury College Field House to witness Burr and Burton's first basketball state championship. The *Bennington Banner* sports editor called it a "rags to riches tale" and wrote that "... the Manchester squad at the beginning of the season looked on paper to be one of the better teams in the rough and tough Marble Valley League but it was not generally anticipated they would finish the season with anything more than a possible playoff bid."

The Bulldog "Iron Five" gave fans a thrilling evening as they fought with determination, finally besting Northfield 64-56 for the state crown.

The chants of war protesters may have seemed like distant thunder at the school on the hill, but Burr and Burton students were no less affected than others across the country – or less immune to the tragedy of war.

In 1967, Jim Dooley, '60, was piloting a Skyhawk fighter bomber on a dangerous bombing run over the railroad yards in the North Vietnam city of Haiphong when he was hit by enemy anti-aircraft fire. His plane went down in the mouth of the Haiphong River. There were no radio transmissions or sightings of a parachute. Jim was listed as "missing in action" until the end of the war six years later when his classification was changed to "presumed killed in action."

While a student at Burr and Burton from 1956 to 1960, he played baseball and football, and was a member of the ski team. Jim also enjoyed drama and acted in several productions put on by the Drama Club. In his spare time, he worked as a mechanic for his father, who owned Manchester Motors, a local Ford dealership.

Jim Dooley, Class of 1960, Lieutenant Commander, U. S. Naval Reserves 1942-1967

During an emotional decade, Mr. Henry kept the school on an even keel. Discussion forums were held, speeches made, and mock elections were organized around the traditional high-school preoccupations of football games, dances, and examinations. In 1969, when Al Henry retired after twenty-five years as headmaster, the Vermont Headmasters Association sent him a quote from John Ruskin which they felt perfectly reflected his philosophy of education: "Education does not mean teaching people what they do not know, it means teaching them to behave as they do not behave. . . . It is painful, continual, and difficult work to be done by kindness, by watching, by warning, by precept, and by praise, but above all – by example."

Lt. JAMES E. DOOLEY

Manchester Navy Pilot Missing

MANCHESTER — Lt. (j.g.) James E. Dooley, 24, Navy pilot with the 7th Fleet Carrier Oriskany, is "missing in action" in Vietnam, according to notification received by his parents, Mr. and Mrs. Henry E. Dooley of Manchester Center.

A Navy officer from Dartmouth College brought the tragic news to the Dooley family Monday afternoon. Lt. Dooley in the Navy for three years, has been in the Far East since July.

Friends in California who have received the same notice as the Dooleys believe that the plane went down Sunday during one of the many strikes in which the local pilot has been involved.

A graduate of Burr and Burton Seminary and Boston College, Lt. Dooley completed Navy Officers Candidate School in Newport, R.I. and was then assigned to Pensacola, Fla. He was stationed at Lamour Navy Base, Calif., before going to Vietnam.

Only last week Lt. Dooley was reported in the New York Times to have been one of the fliers who in direct hits caused heavy damage to a Haiphong-Kienan early warning radar site eight miles south of the port city.

Sarah Given Larson at the dedication of the new wing in 1965

In 1953, Headmaster Henry told the Board of Trustees that an enrollment of 165 students was the ideal number for the present facilities. By 1963, the enrollment had grown to close to 200 and the school's buildings were no longer adequate. There was talk in the community of building a union high school. Fortunately for Burr and Burton, one of the "preservers" mentioned by Loveland Munson fifty years earlier came forward in the nick of time.

Sarah Given Larson was a great friend of Headmaster Al Henry. The daughter of John LaPorte and Irene (Heinz) Given, longtime Manchester Village summer residents, and the granddaughter of H. J. Heinz, Mrs. Larson maintained a residence in Manchester for many years and was quietly generous to numerous community groups.

Through the Irene Heinz Given and John LaPorte Given Foundation, Mrs. Larson donated to the school a grant of $250,000 to build the classroom annex fondly known as the "New Wing." The brick structure replaced the wooden annex which had been added to Seminary Building in 1912 and provided modern classrooms.

St. Paul's, Manchester's first Roman Catholic Church, was consecrated in 1896.

After renovation work was completed, the former church became known as the Practical Arts Building. In 2002, the name was changed to Larson Hall, in honor of Mrs. Larson's generosity to the school.

Mrs. Larson made her gifts in memory of her parents and her brother John. In 1968, she helped Burr and Burton purchase and renovate the former Catholic Church on Seminary Avenue to provide much-needed new classroom space.

Larson Hall is home to the Special Services Department at Burr and Burton and the woodworking classes. It was renovated in 2000 with substantial support from the Preservation Trust of Vermont and the Freeman Foundation.

The boys' soccer team won its first state championship in 1979.

1970	Students hold protest demonstration
1975	New gymnasium dedicated to E. H. Henry
1993	Original 1913 gymnasium transformed into arts center
1998	Smith Center for Science and Communications opens
1999	The Board of Trustees votes to change name to Burr and Burton Academy
2004	Rowland Center completed
2005	175th Anniversary Celebration

V *Tradition & Transformation*

1970 – 2005

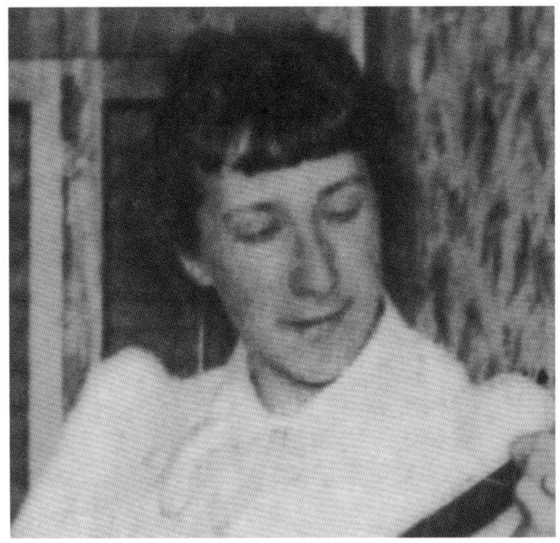

Pauline Batchelder Campbell, Class of 1894

W. H. Shaw, teacher and trustee

James B. Campbell, Class of 1928

Doug Shaw, Class of 1947

Ed Campbell, Class of 1970

Andy Shaw, Class of 1975

The Campbell family can trace its relationship to the school back to the 1850s. Pauline B. Campbell's grandfather was a teacher at Burr Seminary and her father was a graduate and a trustee. Her son James also served as a trustee for many years and his son Ed is a current trustee.

Walter Shaw, teacher and trustee, married Esther Graves '13. All five of their children were graduates and son Doug served as president of the Board of Trustees. His son Andy continues the family tradition as a trustee.

Howard Wilcox, Class of 1932

Elizabeth West Bartlett, Class of 1925

Ron Wilcox, Class of 1957

Landy Bartlett, Class of 1957

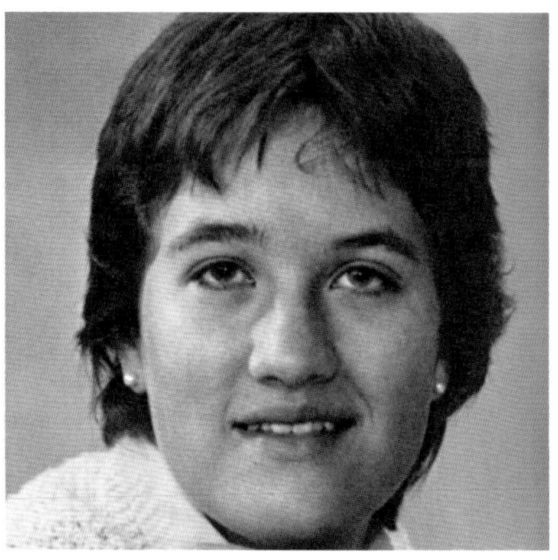

Sarah Wilcox, Class of 1989

Elise Bartlett, Class of 1994

The Wilcox family have been dairy farmers in Manchester since the early 1900s. Their cattle graze on the same land south of the village where the first settlers built their homes. Dozens of Wilcox family members are graduates of Burr and Burton and several have served as trustees. Ron Wilcox has been the official basketball game scorekeeper for both boys' and girls' teams for over twenty years.

Elizabeth West was the daughter of Frederick H. West '92 of Dorset. She and her husband Clay Bartlett were among the founding artists of the Southern Vermont Arts Center. Their son Landy graduated from Burr and Burton in 1957. The tradition continued with her grandchildren, Elise '94 and Blair Bartlett '96.

In November 1970, Burr and Burton students staged the school's one and only protest demonstration – not against the Vietnam War, but in response to the dismissal of the football coach, Victor Crump. The students alerted the press in advance of their original plan to march from the school to the office of the Board of Trustees President Doug Shaw '47. Forewarned, Shaw short-circuited their plans by arriving on campus. He and the headmaster, Neal McLaughlin, attempted to explain the situation to the approximately 125 students who demanded a meeting be held with student representatives present. Shaw agreed and the twelve-minute peaceful protest was over. The Board of Trustees met for five hours that evening and again with students the next day. Headmaster McLaughlin called it an "unfortunate misunderstanding."

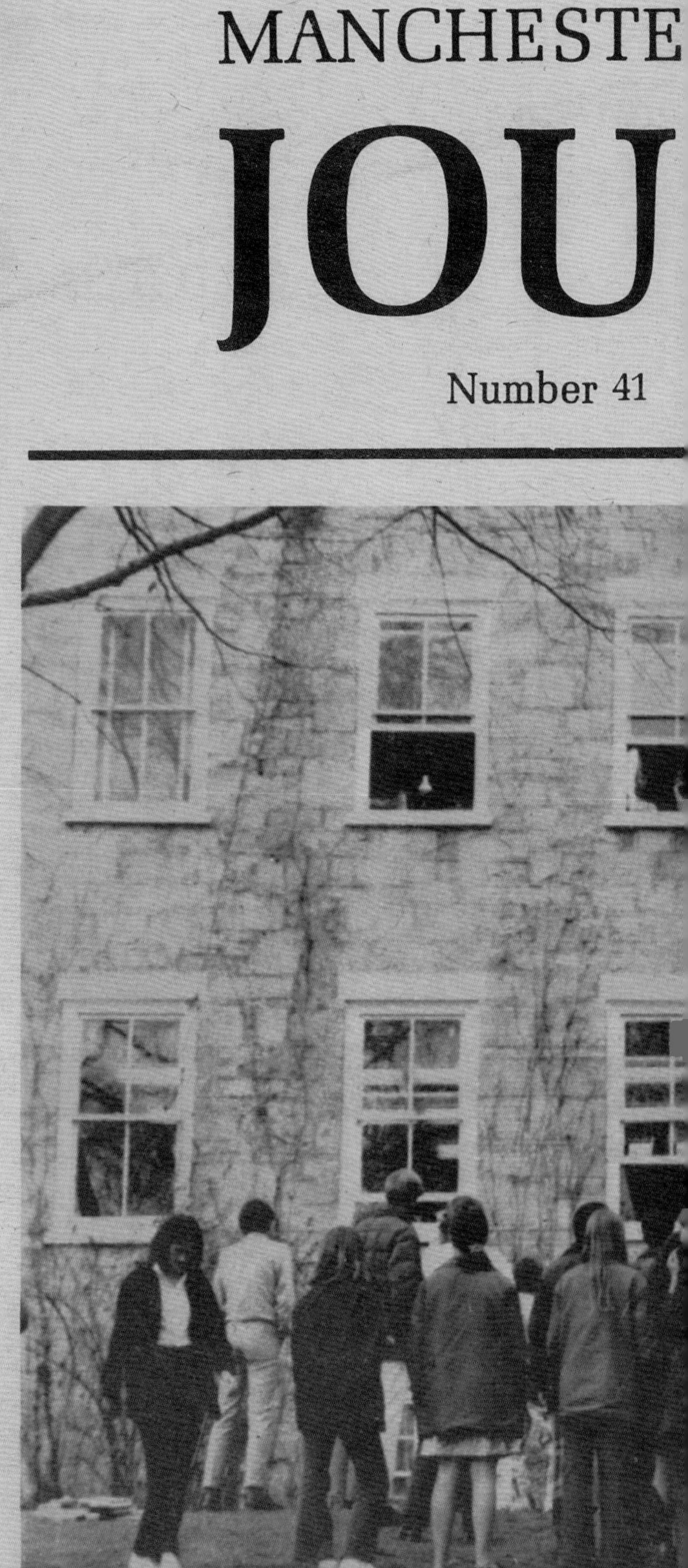
MANCHESTE
JOU
Number 41

The tradition of restricting the marble front steps to members of the senior class began in the 1960s. According to legend, the intention was to cut down on the number of times the front door was opened in winter, allowing blasts of icy air to envelope the front office staff. This was not the first restriction placed on the original entrance. In the 1920s, only the boys were permitted to use the front door, while the girls had their own entrance on the south side of Seminary Building.

RNAL

The Journal will appear on Wednesday next week

Volume 110 Manchester, Vermont November 19, 1970 Fifteen Cents

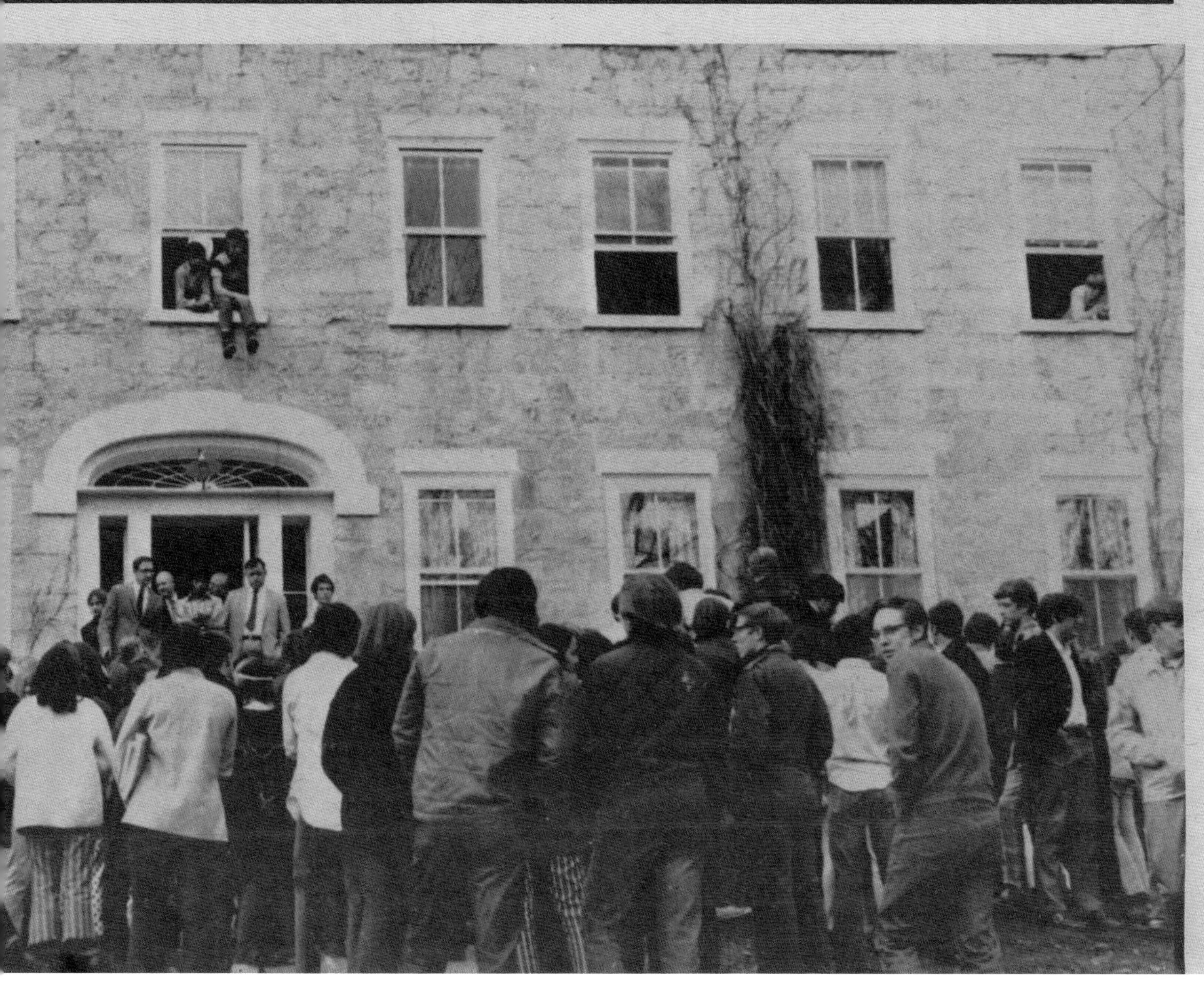

The most significant challenges that face the school now [1993] are similar to those faced by the Seminary in 1978, when I first took office: maintaining independence amidst significant pressure to be more public, securing resources to ensure adequate facilities, and seeking to set high academic standards without risking the future of those students whose goal is simply to finish high school with dignity.

Headmaster Robert G. Kennedy, 1978-1993

Burr and Burton was alive with spirit and activities. It was a wonderful balance of serious, meaningful learning, treasured traditions, and an exciting social culture. I loved it so much I returned!

John Wright, Class of 1966 and
Social Studies teacher since 1970

During my four years at Burr and Burton there was always a great sense of family between faculty and students. We were a small school so everyone knew each other and we were always there for one another.

Jackie Bell Sargood, Class of 1970

The highlight of my high-school career was winning the first-ever state championship in girls' basketball in 1980. I can still vividly remember the escort into town with police, fire, and rescue trucks, and yelling out the windows and having our wet hair freeze. When we got back to school we stood on the steps of the old gym and sang the alma mater to the hundreds of fans that had made the trek to Barre on the coach buses! The Bennington Banner *headline on Monday morning read "A Weekend of Champions." Our team picture was featured along with the USA men's hockey team that had beaten Russia for the gold medal.*

Kathi Frost Bierwirth, Class of 1981

If I had to pick my favorite years of life so far, I'd have to say it was the years I was at Burr and Burton. So many of us in all classes were so tight. We'd do everything together from playing hackey-sack on the hill during lunch, to toga parties at the quarry on Friday afternoons, to cheering each other on at soccer and field hockey games. So many of my high-school pals are still my best friends today.

Amy Walter Chamberlain, Class of 1985

My involvement with Burr and Burton was more extensive than most as my parents were on staff and I spent a lot of time at the school from age seven on. I grew up running the lines for soccer games, going to all the football games, and being the ball boy for the basketball team. I have fond memories of the camaraderie and school spirit as well as the friendliness of the staff. The student body turned out in large numbers for the games – when I think back to those times, I can still hear the sound of the school bell ringing after victories. Burr and Burton was a special place and I benefited greatly from my years there.

Seth Rice, Class of 1982

We had an open campus when I was at Burr and Burton. If you didn't have a class, you could leave school. This was not very popular with the grown-ups, I think.

Andy Shaw, Class of 1975

Burr and Burton was the beginning of our transition to adult life. We not only got an excellent education but we learned about ourselves, about friendships, and about interactions with others.

Rob Treat, Class of 1982

Don Otis was an excellent chemistry teacher who really made it fun, at least for me. I remember so well that certain look he would give that said, "You don't really want to give that answer, do you?"

Cindy Casey O'Leary, Class of 1974

One of the amazing things I remember about being a member of the Burr and Burton class of 1984 was how we were really in on the ground floor of experiencing computer technology in the schools. During the course of one year, I learned to type on a manual typewriter, and after becoming proficient with the layout of the keyboard and the all-important home row, I moved on to the electric typewriter – the speed and ease on our fingers was remarkable. From there I was able to take perhaps one of the first computer classes at Burr and Burton. A small group of students worked with Mr. Brandt down in the lower level of the library. There were just a few large computers down in that basement at the time, but it really was the start of computer technology education at Burr and Burton.

Kathy Bowen Harrington, Class of 1984

Thinking back on my time at Burr and Burton fills me with many warm memories. From a gymnasium packed to capacity with community members cheering on the basketball team, to annually preparing baskets and delivering them to families in need over the holidays, the unconditional support was evident. Support for the community by the school, support for the school by the community, teachers and faculty supporting the students, and most important, students positively supporting each other. This lesson was a wonderful gift that I carry forward with me to this day.

Denise Kilburn Tuttle, Class of 1980

The opening of the E. H. Henry gym was such an exciting time for all of us. The players for both girls' and boys' basketball programs were really happy to have their own gym. People probably don't remember that we had to use the MES gym for both practices and games.

George "GG" Allard
Boys' basketball coach, 1978-1982

When I was a Burr and Burton student in the early 1970s, Manchester was a small, quiet town where everybody knew everybody and nobody locked their doors. About twelve of us spent a lot of time together. If we decided to go camping for the weekend or on a trip to a concert at UVM, we would meet on Main Street at the appointed hour and pile from our individual cars and trucks into a couple of cars for the trip. We would leave the others parked on Main Street, with the doors unlocked and the keys in the ignition. A day or two later, we would pile back out of the two cars, get into those we had left on the street, turn the key, and drive home.

Seth Bongartz, Class of 1972

The rapport between the students and the teachers made the educational experience that much more personal. Henry Harson taught English and he was not only a great teacher but a wonderful man. Bob and Bev Leslie were also very caring teachers.

Wendy Comar, Class of 1980

For a new student entering my junior year just after I had lost my father, high school could have been rough, but Headmaster Houghton Pearl and teachers John Wright and Bev Leslie really made sure I was looked after. This is what I remember most about Burr and Burton – the caring attitude of the faculty.

Wendy Newhouse Gawlik, Class of 1977

It's easy to get nostalgic when I think about those times. The town and village had a cozier feel and it seemed like everyone knew each other. I loved my time at the school, enjoyed meaningful relationships with students, teachers, coaches, and others who worked at the school. The folks in town really rallied around the Bulldogs' sports back then and that will always remain a special memory for me.

Dave Shehadi, Class of 1977

Dedication ceremonies for the E. H. Henry Physical Education Center, 1976

The school faced a host of difficulties in the early 1970s. Enrollment was dropping off and the local economy was stalled. Deficits plagued the annual operating budgets and there was serious talk of taking the school public. The buildings were growing increasingly inadequate and the lack of a proper gymnasium drew criticism from state education leaders. The need for a new gymnasium had been recognized for many years as the basketball teams had been forced to use the Manchester Elementary School gym ever since its opening in 1951. In 1975, the Board of Trustees made two important decisions: They voted to keep Burr and Burton independent and to go forward with the construction of a new gym and cafeteria. The new buildings would be funded through a capital campaign. The gym was named in honor of Headmaster E. H. Henry and dedicated on December 4, 1976. The total cost was $450,000.

Basketball was the first organized sport offered for girls at Burr and Burton. The first girls' team played a full season in 1914, enjoying the new gymnasium completed in 1913. In 1980, the girls' varsity basketball team won their own state championship, their first in the E. H. Henry Center.

Championship jacket for the 1977 boys' basketball state championship team presented to team members by Coach GG Allard at a community banquet held in April 1977 to honor the team.

The brand-new gymnasium proved to be a harbinger of good luck as the boys' basketball teams enjoyed a string of winning seasons in the years immediately after its completion. In 1977 Burr and Burton took its third – and second consecutive – state basketball championship, defeating Woodstock High School. Football had been discontinued for lack of funds in 1975, but by this time the sport of soccer had become the game of choice for many students.

The Arts Challenge Campaign, undertaken in 1992, was directed toward realizing a long-held dream of a theater space for drama and music instruction, and a gallery devoted to the fine arts. After the new gymnasium was built, the old gym was named Alumni Hall. It continued to be used for dramatic and musical performance, but it was badly in need of renovation. The trustees originally looked at building an entirely new facility, but decided for financial reasons to work with the existing building. Architectural plans incorporated parts of the original fittings into the new design and seating was designed for two hundred and forty people. Originally called the Smith Center for the Arts in 1993, the name was changed in 1998 when the Smith Center for Science and Communications opened. The new name of Riley Center for the Arts recognized the generous support of Barbara Riley Levin and Gerald M. Levin to *Campaign 2001.*

THE ROBERT E. & MARGARET SMITH CENTER FOR THE ARTS

Dedication
May 13, 1993

1995 SUMMER EVENTS
at the

THE ROBERT E. & MARGARET SMITH CENTER FOR THE ARTS

at Burr and Burton Seminary Manchester, Vermont

Saturday June 24	Vermont Tenor **John Thade**
Friday & Saturday July 7 and 8 8 pm	**"Forever Plaid"** presented by Sh stoppers. Music from the Fabul Fifties. A benefit for Burr and B Seminary's Annual Fund.
Monday July 10 through Friday July 21	**Circus Minimus.** A two-week shop in circus skills for childre 6-13. Taught by Kevin O'Keef mer co-director of the Big Ap cus School.
Wednesdays July 12-August 9 3-5 pm	**Manchester Music Festiv Classes.** Celebrated profe teaching young musicians
Saturdays July 15-August 12 7:30 pm	**Manchester Music Festi Artists Concerts.** Inform mances featuring the yo cians studying in Manch summer.
Wednesday July 26 8 pm	**Bayfest.** British-Ameri Theater Festival.
Sunday August 6	

You are cordially invited to attend the Burr and Burton Seminary Board of Trustees

Outdoor Dedication Of The ROBERT E. AND MARGARET SMITH CENTER FOR THE ARTS

Four Handed Piano
JANE WOOD & REV. RICHARD RINGENWALD
Cello and Piano
MICHAEL RUDIAKOF & RON LEVY
Reception with the Artists
Jazz Quartet
SARA KROHN, JEFFREY LEVINE, MARJE ROOEN & RUTH SKUSE

Thursday, May 13th, 7:30 p.m.
RSVP Ellen Wilcox 362-1775

The old gymnasium was the setting for dances, theatrical productions, and musical performances from its opening in 1913. Community groups were always welcome to use the gym for events and concerts, and this did not change with the renovation. The new stage and improved acoustics made it an ideal space for musical events. Among the many artists and orchestras who have performed on the new stage, the Manchester Music Festival has been holding its Young Artists Concerts and Master Classes there for thirty years.

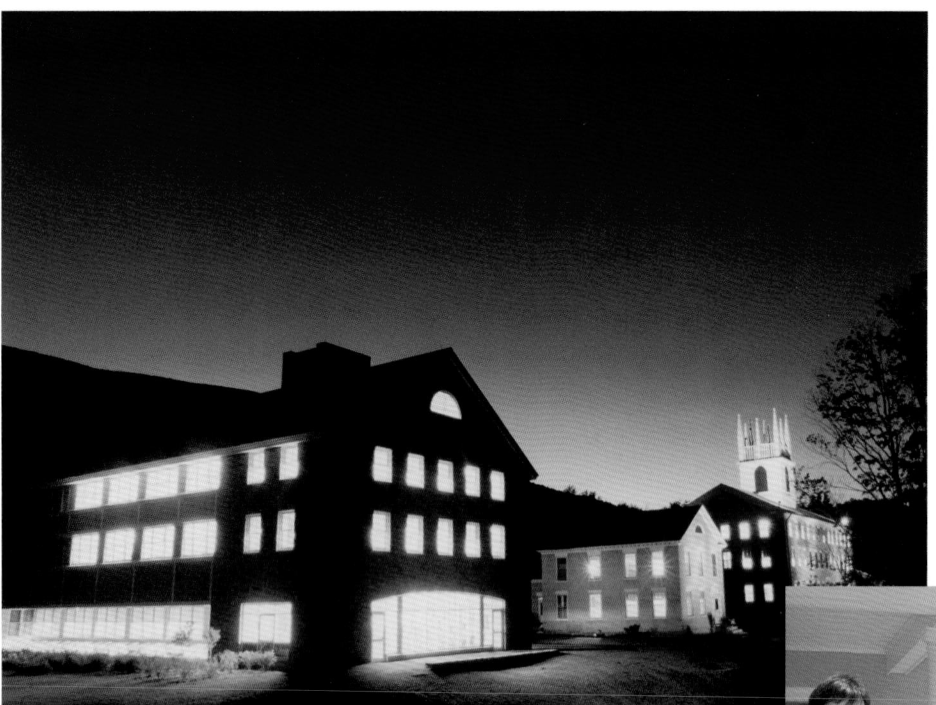

The Smith Center for Science and Communication

Headmaster Charles W. Scranton with Mr. and Mrs. Robert Smith on dedication day for the Smith Center for Science and Communications

When Charles W. Scranton arrived as the twenty-ninth headmaster in 1993, the library in Seminary Building featured only a handful of computers and the science labs were thirty years old. As enrollment, which had declined during the 1980s, began to increase steadily in the 1990s, adequate classroom space became a serious concern. By this time it was clear that computers would be necessary equipment in education as well as in business. The trustees and members of the administration developed a campus master plan to address the challenges faced by the school if it wished to maintain its academic status. In 1996, Burr and Burton received its single largest gift in its history when Mr. and Mrs. Robert Smith donated $3 million to the implementation of the master plan.

On May 15, 1998, Burr and Burton formally dedicated the Smith Center for Science and Communications with Mr. and Mrs. Robert Smith, students, trustees, parents, and friends present. This building represented a momentous transformation for the school as it not only provided much-needed new science laboratories but also a rich infusion of information technology. The students now had access to hundreds of computers and the campus was completely wired, even the original Seminary Building. The Jonathan Levin Center in the lower level, a gift from Barbara Riley Levin and Gerald Levin, provided students with a television studio, video cameras, and professional editing stations. Vermont Public Radio chose Burr and Burton as the home for its southern Vermont studio in 2002.

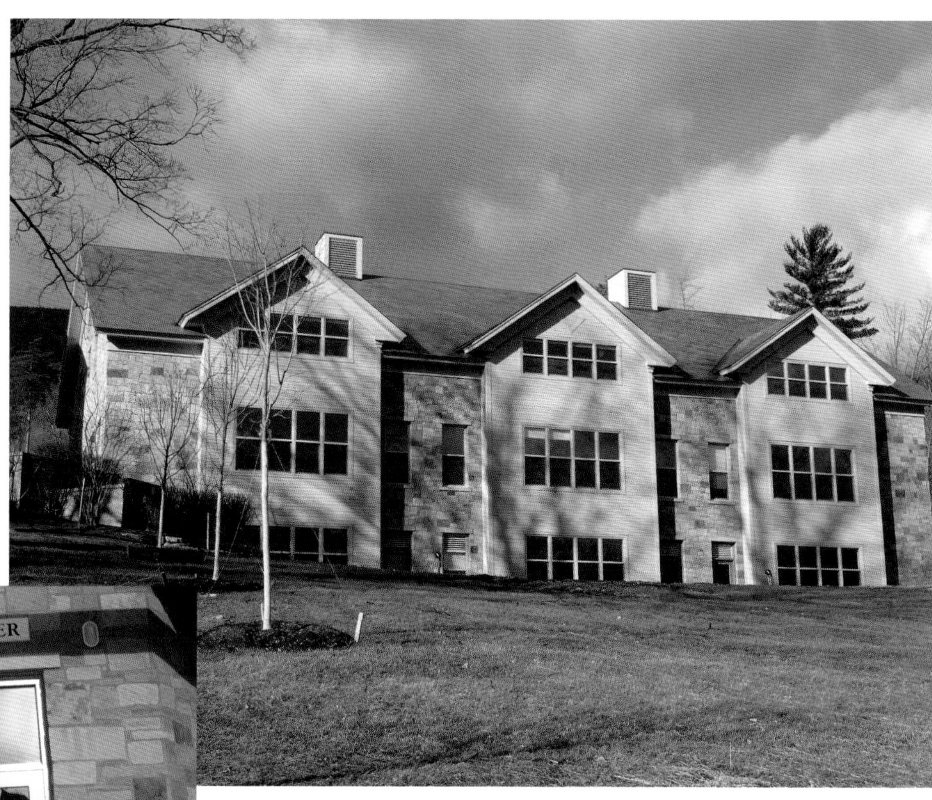

The Rowland Center, 2004

Board Chair Jack Philips (left) and Headmaster Chuck Scranton (right) with trustee Barry Rowland and his wife Wendy, who helped the school realize its dreams for new art studios, foreign language classrooms, and cafeteria

As enrollment continued to grow, the need for more classrooms and renovation to existing buildings became critical. In 2003 the trustees once again undertook a capital campaign to ensure adequate facilities would be provided for future students. *The Campaign for Burr and Burton* was the largest and most successful fundraising effort undertaken by the school in its history. The first of several objectives in the campus master plan to be realized, the new Rowland Center building opened in November 2004, beginning the year-long 175th anniversary celebrations. As the school moves into the final quarter of its second century, it has never been better poised to realize its educational mission. Though its days of being surrounded by a pasture are long gone, the original 1832 limestone building with its spired bell tower is more than ever the symbol of a Vermont community's success.

Enrollment began a steady climb in the early 1990s, nearly doubling from 350 in 1993 to 640 in 2005. During these years, both the boys' and the girls' soccer teams were perennial favorites for state championships. The sport of lacrosse was introduced in 1998 and, after a two-decade hiatus, football returned as a varsity sport in 1999, thanks to the volunteer efforts and financial support of local alumni and business leaders.

Burr and Burton Aca
educate its students, mo
for a life of responsibilit

demy's mission is to

rally and intellectually,

, integrity, and service.

Photo Credits

All photographs and documents are from the archives of Burr and Burton Academy unless noted below:

Endpapers and page 8: Courtesy of Lawrence Wilcox '38
Page 14: Photo by Geoffrey Woodward
Page 15: Photo by Geoffrey Woodward
Page 24: Courtesy of Mr. and Mrs. Richard Lyman
Page 26 (left): From the *Descendants of Josiah Burton*
Page 26 (right): Courtesy of the Manchester Historical Society
Page 27 (left): Courtesy of Mr. and Mrs. Richard Lyman
Page 29: Courtesy of the Manchester Historical Society
Page 28-29: Courtesy of the Vermont Statehouse
Page 34 (left): Courtesy of the American Museum of Fly Fishing
Page 35: Courtesy of the American Museum of Fly Fishing
Page 36 (right): Courtesy of the Manchester Historical Society
Page 37 (left): Courtesy of the Manchester Historical Society
Page 40: Courtesy of the Manchester Historical Society
Page 46: Courtesy of the First Congregational Church, Manchester
Page 47: Courtesy of the Manchester Historical Society
Page 63 (center): Courtesy of the Manchester Historical Society
Page 63 (right): Courtesy of the Dorset Historical Society
Page 77: Courtesy of the Manchester Historical Society
Page 78-79: Courtesy of Doug Shaw '47
Page 84: Courtesy of Mildred Wilcox Orton '28
Page 88: Photo by Clara Sipprell
Page 93: Courtesy of Orland Campbell
Page 93: Courtesy of the Southern Vermont Arts Center
Page 98-99: Courtesy of Peter Henry '60
Page 103: Courtesy of Stan Wilbur '58
Page 108: Photo by Dean Polis
Page 111: Courtesy of Ron Wilcox '57
Page 113: Courtesy of Doug Shaw '47
Page 120: Photo by Dean Polis
Page 120: Photo by Gary Baker '72
Page 121: Photo by Brian Gawlik
Page 121: Photo by Gary Baker '72
Page 123: Photo by Dean Polis
Page 124-125: Photo by Hubert Schriebl

Burr and Burton Academy acknowledges with deepest appreciation the generous underwriting support for the printing of this book provided by Peter Henry '60 and Dorothy Peirce, Richard and Katherine Malley, Barbara and Michael Powers '60, Arden and Chuck Scranton, and Derry and Judy McCormick Taylor '57.

Acknowledgments

Our profound gratitude to all those who helped to make this book possible. We especially wish to thank Lawrence Wilcox '38 for the incomparable gift to the archives of the extensive photograph collection assembled by his mother Grace Root Wilcox '17.

Our thanks also to Mary Bort '44, curator of the Manchester Historical Society, for her invaluable assistance and support, and to Nancy H. Otis for her generous support and permission to use her historical essays first published in 1958 in the *Manchester Journal*. A special thanks to Dorothy Peirce, 175th Anniversary coordinator, and Wendy Newhouse Gawlik '77 for editorial assistance.

Our deepest appreciation especially to the many alumni who participated in the research including Elaine Griffith Nawrath '34, Roger Griffith '37, Doug Shaw '47, Mike McCooey '53, Ron Wilcox '57, Mike Powers '60, Peter Henry '60, Ed Campbell '70, Andy Shaw '75, and Elise Bartlett '94. Ben Beers '61 generously lent us valuable archival items for this book.

We are grateful to Mr. and Mrs. Richard Lyman for permission to access the Reverend Dr. Joseph D. Wickham's papers in the Yale University archives; to David Schutz, curator of the Vermont Statehouse, for permission to use the image of the 5th Regimental flag which is on permanent display in the Statehouse; Brian Knight, Hildene curator; and the American Museum of Fly Fishing for use of the Orvis family photos.

For their gracious professional advice and support, we are most grateful to Randall Perkins, Barbara and Ed Morrow, and Derry Taylor.

We are very honored that award-winning photographer and author Peter Miller '51 graciously provided us with the exclusive photograph created for the limited edition of this book.